LIFE BEGINS
AT
EIGHTY

A Life of Love, Music and Laughter

Virginia Bathurst Beck

Order this book online at www.trafford.com
or email orders@trafford.com

Most Trafford titles are also available at major online book retailers.

Printed in the United States of America.

ISBN: 978-1-4269-9436-4 (sc)
ISBN: 978-1-4269-9435-7 (hc)
ISBN: 978-1-4269-9434-0 (e)

Library of Congress Control Number: 2011915962

Trafford rev. 06/18/2012

 www.trafford.com

North America & international
toll-free: 1 888 232 4444 (USA & Canada)
phone: 250 383 6864 ✦ fax: 812 355 4082

DEDICATIONS

TO MY ENTIRE FAMILY WHO ENCOURAGED ME THROUGH IT ALL.

My husband—Daniel M. Beck

My daughter—Cheryl R. Adkins
My son—Daniel R. Beck
My son—Steven M. Beck
(My children all helped me with the computer)

My Grandson—Daniel R. (DJ) Adkins
My Grandson—John M. Adkins (deceased)
My Grandson—Charles J. Adkins

MY PRIDE AND JOYS

My Great Grandson—Derrick Adkins
My Great Grandson—Zachary J. M. Adkins

(Do you notice the 8 come up again in our descendants?)

I would also like to dedicate this book to my sister, Anna Louse Harvey, who wrote mainly poetry. She died before her book could be accomplished. "Poodie" this is for both of us.

PROLOGUE

I always wanted to write a book but felt that I didn't have time. I always had something else that took priority. I worked after school all through high school. Then in college I worked to pay my tuition. You see I have earned about 80 credits while attending 8 colleges. It would take me about 8 years to graduate, and I don't know if I have that long. I have things to do though that would cover 18 years.

I have had 8 different careers. I've been a factory worker, a waitress, a housekeeper, a secretary, a sales person, a Telephone Sales Representative, a carnival worker (my nephew owns a carnival) and a Beauty Operator when electric permanents were in. It seems that everything in my life includes 8s, 18s, or 80. Thank goodness I didn't have 8 children. 3 were enough to keep me busy. There were 8 people in my immediate family and the first house we built in Blair was 865 North Tenth Avenue.

I have written something all my life. I have written skits for PTA, skits for my TOPS CLUB, Letters to the Editor, and poetry just for my own amusement and for the amusement of my friends. I wrote *Rap* before it became popular.

When I was 80 we moved our winter retirement home from Zapata, Texas to Port St. Joe, Florida. It was there that I launched my first column for the Star News Paper. Two years later I began writing a column for my home town paper, The Pilot Tribune in Blair, Nebraska. Two years after that I launched a column for the Zapata County News in Zapata, Texas. We had wintered there for 18 years, 10 as *snowbirds* and 8 as *residents*. There's that 8 again.

Suddenly it occurred to me that I had already written a book. It was contained within the hundreds of columns I had created. There was material there for 8 books if I wanted to write a series. YES!
OH BOY I have written 2 books from my columns. First there was "LIFE BEGINS AT EIGHTY" published in 2011 and now "PUSHIN' NINETY" which will be published any day now

"E N J 0 Y!"

End of The Trail

Virginia Bathurst Beck

This is the heading for the first column I wrote. It was for the Star Newspaper in Port St. Joe, Florida. I was 81 years old at the time. I was ecstatic to say the least. I didn't feel or look 81 but I was.

The End of the Trail

Virginia Bathurst Beck

Two years later I started a second column in Blair Nebraska where we had lived for 50 years. I knew most everyone who lived there and I loved the feed back I got from them. This heading was used by the Pilot Tribune Newspaper.

Back to the Border

Two years after that I started "BACK TO THE BORDER" for the Zapata News in Zapata.Texas. After we retired this was our winter home. We lived there winters for 18 years then moved to Florida where our son, Dan lived.

Virginia B. Beck
Back to the Border

Danny   Steve   Cheryl
My two guys and a doll

CHAPTER ONE

THE DEPRESSION YEARS

These are my three children at 3, 1 and 5 years of age. The clothes that they have on are all handmade except for their shoes and socks. Their blouses and shirts are made from feed sacks. Their trousers and jumper were made from my husbands old pants.

MY MEAGER BEGINNING

Well here I am finally launching my column-writing career. I was a long time getting here but I am here to stay—that is if ya'all will have me. I'll not tell you how long that trip took because then you'd know how young I am. Let's just say I'm somewhere between 29 and *'you don't want to know.'*

GREAT DEPRESSION

I was born in Sioux City, Iowa in the clutches of the Depression. I was the fifth of six children. For those of you who are too young to know what the Depression was, I'll explain that it was the time when a quarter pound of hamburger could feed a family of eight. Mom would make a big kettle of gravy with the ground beef for flavoring. She then would make a slew of biscuits and boil a half-peck of potatoes. That would be our supper. To celebrate occasionally we had mutton chops that sold for five cents per pound and served them with mashed potatoes.

NAVY BEANS

We frequently ate Navy beans. The bean soup was flavored with pork hocks or slab bacon and seasoned with onions and spices. Our desserts didn't include ice cream or candy but rather simple things like bread with margarine and apple butter. The margarine came in a white block like lard. It was in a plastic bag that included a yellow capsule to break and color it like butter. Since rice was cheep and apples free for the picking, we often had rice and apple pudding for dessert.

At the end of the day the dairies parked their trucks on our street with their left over milk in big containers. Anyone could bring a jug and fill it free. We drank a lot of milk!

DIET AND EXERCISE

In spite of our limited diet, we all grew up pretty healthy probably because our diets included plenty of milk, fruits and vegetables. Those were the cheap foods that our limited finances could afford. Most fatty meats were thus eliminated. I can't remember there being any fast-food restaurants around to eat at. Every where we went we walked, therefore got plenty of exercise. None of us were over or under weight.

GHETTO

We didn't realize that we were poor, and by today's standards we lived in a ghetto. It was just our neighborhood. We didn't have much of anything except plenty of love and guidance from our parents. That's really what counted in the long run. I wouldn't have changed my beginnings for anything.

JOKE OF THE WEEK

Money doesn't make you happy, but it may quiet your nerves.

WAY BACK WHEN

'HEY THAT'S GOOD'

I always wanted to be a writer ever since – well way back when I wrote a few things for my high school paper. Some people (let me rephrase that) at least one person who read my writing said, "Hey that's good." Thus I was encouraged to further effort and wrote more for my high school and college papers.

I WAS ON MY WAY

However a funny thing happened on the way to my literary fame and fortune. You see I met this guy and married him. *SIDETRACKED!* Soon along came a couple of "Little Guys and a Doll." *FURTHER OFF THE TRACK"* . Every time I wanted to reach for my pen, I had to reach instead for a diaper for one of my "Little Guys" or sort a load of laundry, or cook a meal or take my "Doll" to ballet lessons.

EXPENSES – EXPENSES

I kept telling myself I could wait. My little ones wouldn't be young forever. When they grew up I promised myself that I would fight my way through the clutter and find my pen—and I did. But alas! I used it to write out job applications as "my gal" was ready for college and we needed extra income to meet expenses. My job with the telephone co. which was to have lasted only a few years, stretched into 20 , while I used my pen to write checks for college tuition, gas for commuting and retirement funds.

REAL ESTATE IN ZAPATA

Finally, as they say, "all things come to he who waits." After the "chicks flew the coop", we were free to spend as much leave time and vacation as we wanted in the sunny south. We bought real estate in Zapata, T.X. on Falcon Lake where my husband's uncles, Elmer and Albert Spann lived.

There I met this guy, Bob McVey, the Editor of the Zapata News at that time. When I showed him some of my writing, he said "Hey that's good". With those familiar words he made a friend for life. From then on I wrote for McVey in several capacities. I wrote an area column and edited the paper. After 15 years we moved from Zapata to Port St. Joe, Florida for our winter home because of my husband's health. My son Dan already lived there.

WROTE 3 COLUMNS

I have started 2 columns since I left Zapata, one in Port St. Joe, Florida and one in Blair, Nebraska. I'm really looking forward to writing a column for all my friends in Zapata and those friends I've yet to meet.

Thinking back, I do remember who originated those fateful words, "Hey that's good." IT WAS MOTHER.

(As I write this book I am now writing for today's Zapata News Editor, Karran Westerman.)

JOKE OF THE MONTH

A dog is a man's best friend because he wags his tail instead of his tongue.

MEMORY LANE

SPRING CLEANING

Little did I know what would happen when I started spring-cleaning? I'm overcome with "stuff" and needed to rid myself of some of it. I was going to go through everything in our garage and see what I could throw out. "The best laid plans, can go astray". I did fine until I came to a box of pictures among Dan's mother's stuff. I didn't remember seeing them before so I took time out to look.

THE COVERED WAGONS

The first big surprise was a tintype of Dan's mother and her family going from Lincoln to Holt County. There were 5 covered wagons in the train. The box held other Tintypes of his grandparents and his grandpa's family. Great Grandpa and Grandma were stern looking people. It looked like the photographer said for them to "frown" instead of "say cheese" when he took their picture. I wonder if they knew what a line they were starting when they got married.

They had 4 girls and 3 boys. Danny's Mom had 2 boys and 2 girls; Dan and I had 1 girl and 2 boys. We had 3 grandsons (one is now deceased) and 2 great grand sons. That is just one line. Remember there were 6 more lines of them.

NOW SMILE

The wedding pictures are what fascinated me. Great Grandma and Grandpa's were stern, of course. Dan's mom, Effie's and his father, Alvie's picture was a little softer and Danny and I were grinning from ear to ear in ours. There were times later when we wondered what we had to grin about.

THE AGE OF SLACKS

It seemed funny to see the women always in dresses. They didn't dare wear anything that looked like men's clothing. I wore slacks when I was a teenager but we weren't allowed to wear them to school. We couldn't even wear blouses outside our skirts.

I was amazed, when we moved to Blair, that school kids could wear slacks or jeans to school. Danny's mom still wore dresses when we were married. I asked her why she didn't try slacks. She answered that she never thought about it. I told her it was time she did, and bought a pants suit for her birthday. I never saw her in a dress after she started wearing slacks.

SWEET MEMORIES

I enjoyed the trip down memory lane. It, however, made me a little sad to see how many loved ones I'd lost. It made me wonder if I had done all I could for them while they were alive and if I went to see them as often as I could. If your mom and dad are still alive, why not go and look at their old pictures with them. You probably would enjoy it more than after they are gone.

I had an enjoyable day going through the box, but I didn't get much spring-cleaning done. I found this poem among the junk. Here is the cleaned up version.

'A POEM TO ME MUDDER'

**WHEN MY PRAYERS WERE POORLY SAID
WHO TUCKED ME IN MY WIDDLE BED
AND SPANKED ME "B--T" TILL IT WAS RED?
"ME MUDDER"**

**WHO TOOK ME FROM MY COZY COT
AND PUT ME ON THE ICE COLD POT
AND MADE ME "WEE, WEE" IF I COULD OR NOT?
"ME MUDDER"**

BUT WHEN THE MORNING LIGHT HAD
COME
AND IN MY CRIB I'D DRIBBLED SOME
WHO WHIPPED MY TINY LITTLE "B--T"
"ME MUDDER"

WHO WOULD MY HAIR SO GENTLY PART
AND HUG ME GENTLY TO HER HEART
AND SOMETIMES SQUEEZE ME 'TIL I "F--T"?
"ME MUDDER"

WHO LOOKED AT ME WITH EYEBROWS
KNIT
AND GOD "D--MN" NEARLY THROUGH A
FIT
WHEN IN MY SUNDAY PANTS I'd "S--T"
"ME MUDDER"

THE END

CHANGES IN MY LIFETIME

Celebrating our 60 Wedding Anniversary started me to thinking of all the changes I had experienced in my lifetime. Women stayed home years ago and took care of the kids, the house and her husband because then it was a full-time job.

MONDAY

She boiled the water first with lye to get the hardness out. Then she washed the clothes on a washboard and hung them out on a line to dry. Did you know that clothing would freeze dry? She then sprinkled them with water putting wrinkles back in them before ironing. The rest of the day was spent making the beds with clean sheets, cooking and caring for the kids.

TUESDAY

It was always ironing day, heating the solid iron on a cook stove. Everything was ironed as clothing was made of cotton not the wrinkle-resistant blends of cloth that are used today. Then she made beds, cooked and watched kids.

WEDNSDAY

She sewed and darned. They never threw holy socks away, they darned them. Most women, including myself, made most of the kids clothing out of feed sacks. My daughter didn't have a store-bought dress until she was in third grade. Then the wife made beds, cooked and watched kids.

THURSDAY

She baked bread, cakes, pies and cookies, everything that would satisfy a family's stomach cheaply. Then she made beds, cooked and watched the kids.

FRIDAY

She cleaned house: dusted furniture scrubbed the floors and cleaned the windows. Then she made beds, cooked and watched the kids.

SATURDAY

It was bath day. She scrubbed the kids in the washtub. When clean, they accompanied mom to do the shopping. Then she made beds, cooked and watched kids.

SUNDAY

That was church day so they got up early. She made beds, got dinner and put it in a low oven to stay warm. She got herself and the kids ready for church while Dad sat out in the car honking the horn. When everything was cleaned up after dinner SHE HAD TIME OFF!

CHANGES FROM THEN TO NOW

FROM	TO
Smoke Signals	The Telephone
The Horse-pulled Plow	The Tractor
The paper and pencil	The Computer
The washboard and line	Washer and dryer
The checker board	Video Game
The Old cookstove	The Glass Top Stove
The Covered Wagon	The Van
The Horse and Buggy	The BMW

THE BEST CHANGES

I suppose I should say that I miss those days but I just can't. I like it   too well the way it is today. Society no longer expects the women to stay home and take care of the house and her family. She is free to develop her talents at home, if she so chooses, or in the workplace while sharing all that work of cleaning, cooking and caring for the kids with her husband. Our amazing improvement in technology makes housework about half the work that it was. It no longer requires the "lady of the house" to put her every waking hour into keeping up with it.

Hallelujah!!

BONNIE BRADLEY

is the stunning and talented vocalist and Pianist entertaining At Gabriele's Restaurant and Lounge every evening.

CHAPTER TWO

MUSIC, MUSIC, MUSIC

Although all of my family (but me) had beautiful voices, only one my sister, Bonnie (above), sang professionally. She had a voice like an angel. When she sang "The Lord's Prayer" it was moving enough to make an atheist convert.

SONGBIRD

Let me tell you about our family songbird, Bonnie. She was born, I think, after Mom was ready to stop delivering Bathurst children. I was to have been the 'last hurrah', but I wasn't. There weren't so many ways to quit birthing when you were ready in those days.

TWINS

There were just 3 years space between all the other Bathurst kids, and there were 4 years between Bonnie and I. When we were young we were more like twins than sisters born four years apart. The older kids felt that they were too sophisticated to have much to do with us two younger ones, but Bonnie and I stuck together as though we were glued.

SHOW BUSINESS

It wasn't all fun and laughter being glued to someone like Bonnie. She was high spirited and I was always getting her out of one mess or another. For instance, she ran home from school one day at recess and the principal sent me home after her. I guess she never did like school as she quit after 9th grade against mine and my parents objection. When she was just

15 she got a job as usher at a movie theatre. From the beginning she followed some kind of show business.

SHE COULD SING

Her most redeeming quality was that she could sing. I mean she *could really sing*. That family chorus that I was never allowed to join took her in. Soon she became lead singer. I guess singing was her thing. The chorus sang 4 part harmony and when they sang "Whispering Hope" her clear sweet voice rang out above all the others. When they sang their closing number, "The Lords Prayer", her rendition brought down the house with applause.

BELLE OF CHICAGO

We were more or less separated when she was first married. She had a daughter by that union, but her happiness soon ended. After 5 years of marriage her husband died.

After that she was left as a single parent with a child to care for. She did it with the only skill she had-- singing. She went back to the entertainment business to support herself and her daughter.

She moved to Chicago with a band and finally became a favorite entertainer in the best lounges in Chicago. Bonnie remarried and a son was born. She was finally divorced and the rest of her life was filled with music and tragedy.

SINGING WITH THE ANGELS

She died at an early age. Her music is gone. The voice that had charmed many people is now silent. It calms me to believe that my *songbird* has flown to *heaven* and is now singing with the angels.

GIVE OUR REGARDS
TO BROADWAY

GIVE OUR REGARDS TO BROADWAY
REMEMBER US TO HERALD SQUARE

When Gina (Vicar) Meizner and her husband William came to Port St. Joe, they did not plan to stay. She wanted to be near her mother until her baby was born and just relax. After that they planned to go back to New York where their careers were flourishing. He was an actor and she had been a clown, a stand up comic, an actress and her directing career was taking off. She even wrote a play, "Fifteen Minutes a Week", which was produced at the 43rd St. Theatre" in New York City.

"I always loved performing and first got the acting bug in college," she said. Her credits now fill an entire page. The most important roles she said she had played were Vivian in "Love, Sex, and The IRS" and Constanze in "Amadeus" at the Kaleidoscope Theatre in Panama City, "Rosencranze and Guildenstern are Dead" on Queens Main Stage. Her husband, William also acted in "Amadeus" and in "The Nerd.

TELL ALL THE GANG ON 42ND STREET
*THAT WE WILL SOON BE THERE

They came for a visit not to stay in Port St. Joe. They missed their careers and their friends in New York. About the time they were due to go back, Gina was devastated with the news that she had breast cancer. She decided to stay here near her mother to fight the cancer, but that wasn't the only reason they stayed. The main reason was that the people in Port St. Joe were so nice that they decided that they would miss them more than her friends in New York. Also she wanted to stay and help Port St. Joe develop a Community Theatre group that would have fun, expose people to Theatre and provide quality entertainment and music locally.

SAY OUR GOODBYES TO BROADWAY
'CUS' WE'VE DECIDED TO UNPACK

So they unpacked everything and set up housekeeping here. Since then they've been involved in the community in various ways. They were both in Dinner Theatres Gina has produced at the Fish House Restaurant in Mexico Beach, and she has performed in many Panama City productions. They are as follows:

Play	Part	
"Red Stocking Review"	Opening Number	Civic Center
"A Marriage Proposal"	Mavis Bell Cox	Dixie Theatre
"Stephanie's Arena"	Stephanie	Dixie Theatre
"The Ice Man"	Mrs. Gorrie	Dixie Theatre
"Lettice and Lovage"	Miss Farmer/tourist	Kaliedoscope
"A Chance Meeting"	Pamela	Martin Theatre
"Single and Proud"	Sylvia/Janet	Martin Theatre
"Sylvia"	Phyllis/Leslie	Martin Theatre

Gina also has taught a class at the Elementary school sponsored by the G.A.L.A. Organization.

WE'RE GOING TO STAY IN PORT ST. JOE *AND WE'RE NEVER GOING BACK*

I've always wanted to go to New York and see all the plays, but I probably never will. It's in my 'someday' file and will probably stay there. However a thought just occurred to me. Why should we go all the way to New York to see plays when with the Meizners we have a little piece of 'BROADWAY' *right in Port St. Joe?*

| Virginia | John | Sheila |
| Beck | Sorenson | Pille |

MUSIC MAKES THE WORLD GO ROUND

At least it has made 'my world go round'. For every phase of my life there has been music that has made my life more enjoyable.

BABY FACE

I told you before that I came from a musical family. Looking back to when I was born, I can just picture the family chorus surrounding me singing 'Baby Face' and 'Welcome to the World'. That is stretching it a bit, but I do remember each part of my life with a song or two.

BABY SONG

I remember Kindergarten and singing 'The Itsy Bitsy Spider went Up the Water Spout'. I considered that a baby song. My older siblings were singing popular songs in 4 part harmony.

When I was about 10 years old 'Red Sails in the Sunset' was popular. I also have fond memories of that time of my Dad playing 'Turkey in the Straw' and 'Red Wing' on the violin.

GLEN MILLER

During my years in high school, Glen Miller was 'IT'. Two of the songs we sang and danced to were 'Blueberry Hill' and 'Kalamazoo'. That was the time of big bands and ballrooms. My part time job was selling tickets at the Box Office of the Skylon Ballroom in Sioux City. I had autographs from Glen Miller, Fats Domino, Tommy Dorsey and all the rest. That autograph book was stolen from my dorm room in college.

Remember 'Smoke, Smoke, Smoke Your Cigarette'. That was playing on the Juke Boxes when Danny and I were courting. 'String of Pearls' and 'In the

Mood' were also popular then. Of course 'To Each His Own' was our song.

THE BEATLES

During our kids teen years there were some good songs: Chubby Checkers and 'The Twist', 'Wild Thing' and 'The Yellow Submarine'. Remember the Beatles you 'Baby Boomers'?

ELVIS

Then Elvis Presley came along and took over the sound waves and my full attention. I liked his early 'jam sessions' better than I did his later works. I must say, even as his health declined, he didn't lose his voice. 'Love Me Tender' and 'Jailhouse Rock' were two of my favorites. A few years ago my husband bought me tapes of Elvis's gospel songs for my birthday. We carry them in the car and play them over and over. They're the best.

SISTER ACT

'Sisters' and 'You Gotta' see Mama Every Night' are two of the songs Sheila Pille and I performed in our 'Sister Act' for Blair Community Theatre years ago. Although I do not have a very good voice, my partner did. She carried me. I guess my music is all in my soul.

The Tenth Anniversary Performance of Blair Community Theatre at Dana College (pictured), was my swan song. However Sheila went on to better things at The Omaha Community Theatre. "Way to go girl'!

LINE DANCING

I may not be able to sing, but I can dance. My line dancing partners in Zapata can testify to that. We had lessons at Lake Front and Four Seasons R. V. Parks and I went to both. Those Western Songs and their rhythm keep going through my head even now. Here in Florida I have to drive 15 miles to dance. With gas what it costs, needless to say:

I DON'T GO VERY OFTEN!

"DREAM A LITTLE DREAM OF ME."

Many different stories are told about dreams. Lots of people believe that they mean something in your life. There have even been many scary stories about dreams, associating them with something bad that is going to happen to you or near you. We have read about people who have seen a dream or a vision of a crime scene and help the police solve their crimes.

MY DREAMS

I cannot say whether these things are true or not. I'm a realist. They are not true of my dreams. Mine are usually about my family. They are strange because they are not about anything that really happened. They are more like watching a movie or TV with them as the stars. If I don't go over my dreams in my mind several times or write them down, I never remember them.

DREAM CLASS

Many times when I wake up, I can't remember dreaming at all. I know that I have dreamed because in a psychology class I took at Dana College, I learned that if you didn't dream you would become psychotic. Many lab experiments have been taken on dreams. Technicians wake volunteers up each time they start to dream. There dreaming was signaled by the fluttering of their eyelids. When they woke those people, they were really disoriented and had other symptoms of psychosis. So all we know for sure is that dreaming must work as a pop off valve for our emotions, so dream away!

UPS AND DOWNS

I also learned in that class that we have different levels of sleep. When you sleep, you have ups and downs from deep sleep to levels where you are barely sleeping. You only remember that you have dreamed if you wake up when you are dreaming in that top level of sleep. I have always been interested in dreams and dreaming. However I do not think that dreams mean anything supernatural. It is just my subconscious mind's way of providing that pop off valve and don't believe they mean anything special. At least they don't to me. I can't answer for other people. If there are those who dream solutions to crimes, and they help the police, more power to them.

ROMANCE

Many romantic songs have been written about dreams. The following are some that I remember:

"Dream a Little Dream of Me", "I'll See You In My Dreams", "Did You Ever See a Dream Walking", "All I Do Is Dream of You", "Listen to the Mocking Bird", "I'm Dreaming Now Of Sweet Hallie", "Dream When Your Feeling Blue" and "Beautiful Dreamer".

JOKES OF THE WEEK

When you wish upon a star... you've got a rather tenuous grip on reality.

Into each life some rain must fall...especially if you left your windows open.

I CAME FROM A MUSICAL FAMILY

I came from a musical family. No one would ever guess that if they heard my off-key warbling in church. My Dad was an accomplished musician. His repertoire was varied, but as a child I couldn't figure out what the right name for his instrument was. When he played "Red Wing", or "Turkey in The Straw", he called it a fiddle. When he played the "Missouri Waltz" or "Over The Waves", he called it a violin. I remember sitting at rapt attention when he played the classical "Spanish Fandango" on the guitar.

BROTHERS

My brothers had a band. The older one played lead guitar and violin while the younger one played the banjo. That was when I learned the songs, "Little Brown Jug", and "Sweet Georgia Brown."

We had a family chorus too. That isn't exactly true. The Bathurst family had a chorus but they wouldn't let me sing because they said I was too young. Getting older didn't help. I never did get in that chorus.

MY CHILDREN ARE MUSICAL

Music runs in my family. My daughter played clarinet in the school band and danced with the band at fairs and other celebrations. My older son taught himself the guitar and played and sang at weddings, funerals and The Community Theatre. I loved the piano. I learned to appreciate classical music from a college roommate who played "Malaguena" and "Clare De Lune" beautifully. When I urged my youngest son to play it he refused. Instead he played the drums. His specialty solo was "Wipe Out".

With this background, I learned to appreciate all kinds of music. I did, that is, until the present generation came along. My grandson's are excellent guitarists who have both played in bands. The older one, D.J., is probably the best musician since my Dad and my son Danny. His son, Zachary, is a close second.

HARDROCK

I feel that D. J.'s talent is being wasted playing in a "Hard Rock Band". This has caused a running battle between us. I told him that I've tried to understand their music but I can't even understand the lyrics.

He answered that I didn't have a reason to brag about our music. He said that he had found a book called: "Great Hits of the Forties" in the dentist's office with these gems listed therein:

SONGS OF MY TIME

*Three Little Fishes –("In a iti, bity, poo fwam free itty fittys and a Mommy fitti too")
*Civilization–("Bingo, bango, bongo-I don't wanta leave the Congo No, no, no, o o o.")
*Mairzy Doats-("Mairzydoats and dozydoats and little lambzeetivy")

"You'd have been better off if you couldn't have understood those baby talk lyrics" he said. I explained that those songs were like live comedy routines to us. He answered "you don't think that my peers take HARD ROCK seriously do you"?

Well he won that argument, but "To Each His Own." My favorite song is still "Mares Eat Oats" and Does Eat Oats and Little Lambs Eat Ivy (the right words). You can like w h a t e v e r !!!

CHAPTER THREE

DOGS, HORSES & CATS

Millie was Steve & Jeannie's dog who has gone to Doggie Heaven. I can't have a favorite among my 3 kids, so she was my favorite among their 3 dogs. When she 'passed on' they adopted Adorable, 'Dorie' for short, to take her place. She can't quite make it, but it isn't for lack of trying.

MILLE

When the Omaha Humane Society officer found Millie, she looked like a big ball of lint waddling down the street. At the shelter, my daughter in law Jeannie, who volunteers there, had to practically shave her to get the mats out of her hair. She carved out to be an eight pound Yorkshire Terrier, black with a silver head and silver paws.

ADOPTIVE

Millie was a perfect adoption candidate, because of her small size, sweet temperament, and large brown eyes. Unfortunately, when they spayed her, disease was found in her kidneys and she was diagnosed as terminal. Right then her adoption chances went from great to zero. The shelter cannot adopt out sick animals so they might have been forced to terminate her immediately.

BIG HEART

But take heart. I learned that there are all kinds of heroes and heroines. In a facility of big hearts, the biggest of all kicked in----Jeanie's! Her work in surgery as well as being an adoption counselor enabled her to take Millie as a foster dog until she recovered from her surgery. Although she and my son, Steve, had already adopted two dogs, they still opened their hearts to Millie and never took her back to the pound.

CANNONBALL RUN

When I met Millie, it was love at first sight. Each time we visit our son and daughter in law; all three dogs run down the hill in front of the house with Millie on their tail like a patrol officer. She throws her twelve pounds against them and nips at their tails as if to knock them out of the race. Millie doesn't have too much control over her bladder and that run usually brings on the water. I just wait until the flood is over and then pick her up, At Jeannie's last birthday party, however, I held her the entire time. So what if I was a little wet when I went home!

OFFICIAL ADOPTION

They finally adopted her formally and made her officially one of the family. When you see how happy Millie is, you know she doesn't realize she is sick. When her bad kidneys finally catch up with her she'll go to "Doggie Heaven" but in her mind she will go RUNNING AND JUMPING ALL THE WAY.

PASSED ON

(Since this column was written, Millie has passed away leaving many happy memories behind. Since then Steve and Jeanie have adopted another dog, Adorable, 'Dorie' for short, to help take Millie's place. She hasn't "TAKEN IT" but not for lack of trying.)

HONORED

Recently Jeannie was honored by THE NEBRASKA HUMAN SOCIETY as Volunteer of the Year. The society stated in their Publication, Tail's Tails, "Jeannie Beck has contributed 2500 hours in three years! She works primarily with the surgical staff and has touched the lives of thousands of animals. "Way to go Jeannie! NHS appreciates your dedication and we know your animals do too."

PET PATTER

Just because we don't have pets now, people jump to the conclusion that we do not like animals. That is far from the truth. We raised cats and dogs along with our children. The kids were taught to love and care for all their animals. I would like to tell you about one of those pets that stands out in my memory as quite unusual.

OUR CAT SAM

I'll admit to you that I always loved dogs, but I didn't have the same fondness for cats. That situation ended when I met SAM. At that time we raised Chocolate Labrador Dogs, so I told the kids that they could not have cats. That was just too much!

FAMOUS LAST WORDS!

While my back was turned Margaret Trisdale's cat had a litter of kittens. Of course my kids wanted one of the cute little darlings. I said NO until my tongue turned dry, and I thought that was the end of it. It was until my oldest son, Daniel, came home carrying the cutest little kitten you ever saw. Margaret, being my son's second mother, felt he should have one, so without my approval, she gave Sam to him. His eyes were big and pleading as he held the cat tight and looked up at me saying please mom PLEASE! PLEASE! PLEASE! What mother could say no to that? So the kitten became Sam and became one of us.

PROBLEM SOLVED

My main objection was not to the cat, but to having a smelly litter box in the house. Therefore we immediately set about house breaking him. We put kitty litter in a cardboard box for him to use and slowly moved it toward and out the back door. Sam followed it. When we finally shut the back door, he would go to the door and scratch to get out to go to his box. We kept moving the box until it was behind the orchard. The cardboard finally disintegrated but Sam kept going out to that area. Those who say that you can't train a cat are wrong. You just need to use a lot of patience in doing it.

THE HUMAN CAT

Sam thought that he was human. He and the kids became very close. They could do anything they wanted with him as long as they were gentle. They even played catch - with him as the ball. We made one mistake. We didn't have him spayed. When he got older, he began to roam coming home intermittently.

Then there was a time that he didn't come home at all. We put the word out to watch for him.

The last sighting we had reported to us was that he was spotted walking down a church isle. The kids said that he must have been on his way to "Cat Heaven" when he disappeared for the last time. It seemed better that way. They could have been right. He deserved it.

MY KINGDOM FOR A HORSE

When I was a kid, I always wanted a horse. Since we lived in the city and my parents had only a small yard, I didn't have much chance of getting one.

RED LIGHTNING

Many times I imagined myself riding like the wind on a fast-footed horse I called "Red Lighting." I was either dashing across the prairie, running from a pack of "wild Indians," or I was chasing a handsome cowboy that looked a lot like Roy Rogers. The Indians never caught me, and I never caught up with the cowboy, but I certainly tried.

When I was growing up, the only horses I rode were "Merry-Go-Round" horses. Later I rode horses at riding stables, but it seems that they always gave me the old slow ones to ride. They were nothing like the "Red Lightning" that I had ridden in my childhood dreams.

ANTIQUE HORSE

But all things come, as they say, to those who wait. I have a nephew, Dennis, who bought an old carnival and replaced the horses on the Carousel with new ones. That left him with a lot of antique wooden horses. Knowing about my love affair with all kinds of horseflesh, he gave me one of those antiques and told me where I could get it restored.

MINI HISTORY

As I waited for my turn to have the horse restored, I studied the origin of the old wooden horses. I found that my horse was made by C. W. Parker at his Wooden Horse Ranch in Leavenworth, Kansas. In his 'Heyday' Parker was the Napoleon of the manufacture of amusement devices. He didn't only make the devices; in 1902 he launched a carnival company under C. W. Parker Amusement. It finally developed in 1916 to Parker's Greatest Shows, probably the most elaborate and pretentious organization ever attempted at that time. It required a train of 35 all steel cars for its transportation.

CAROUSEL

Special features of the plant at Leavenworth was Carry-Us-Alls (Carousels), with the numerous hand painted wooden horses inset with cabochon jewels in the design, mechanical organs, and other devices required in the show business. From Leavenworth the products were shipped to all parts of the world. The Parker Carry-Us-Alls went to the Philippine

Islands, to islands of the tropic seas, to Australia, and to the Southern states.

RESTORED HORSE

I had my horse finished like a sorrel with a red flaming main and tail. The glass jewels I ordered were my family's birthstones: a sapphire an amethyst, two diamonds and a garnet. It has cured my fetish for horses. I've exchanged my riding for looking and it works. Instead of riding a real horse, I just look admiringly at my restored antique Merry-Go-Round" horse.

After reading the story of Charles Parker and the beautiful wooden horses he created, I realize how lucky I am to have one. The man was a creative genius. I have a little bit of history that can never be duplicated.

LADY OF THE HOUSE

OUR FIRST DOG

Whoever coined the phrase dumb animal was not acquainted with our Golden Labrador, Lady. Now either she was brilliant for a dog or I am stupid for a human, as she outsmarted me at every turn.

Lady was two years old when we adopted her, but she took to our family as though she was born into it. Took over our family might be more accurate. Being our first dog it didn't take her long to win the undying devotion of my 3 children and one husband. As for me, I soon discovered that a dog may be a man's best friend, or a boy's, or even a little girl's but certainly not a housewife's.

HER DOMAIN

At that time we lived in the basement of our house and Lady had the run of the unfinished upstairs rooms. This arrangement was fine with her. Our rivalry began when we finished the house and moved upstairs and I attempted to take over her domain. Being of gentle nature, Lady met my every move with passive, yet studied resistance. She followed me around getting in my way and deliberately tripping me. She always slept where I wanted to sweep, or just sat in front of the cupboard door that I wanted to get into. She always watched my every move. When I complained my husband only laughed at my imagination.

LOSING BATTLE

Attempts to keep her out of the living room, and thus keep her gold hair off my green rug, met with more frustrating results. Lady sat in the doorway and howled until the children were all consoling her and friend husband was looking at me as though I was something from another planet. Fearing a family rift with me on the losing side, I gave in. Lady once again had the run of the house and everyone was happy but Mom. Actually I think she was convinced that she was the Lady of the House and I was the imposter.

SHE DIDN'T

As I vacuumed hair off the rug and furniture, I consoled myself with the hope that in the summer she would stay outside (famous last words). *She didn't.* Instead she played hostess and greeted our guests with her nose sticking out between the drapes of the front window and a smile on her NOT SO DUMB COUNTENANCE!

A HORSE IS A HORSE OF COURSE

My 'funny bone' was tickled when I read an article in an Eastern Newspaper some time ago. There was no author's name on the article that I could give credit to here. The article just indicated that it had come from Pennsylvania. So I thought it worth writing about in my own words, so that, if anyone missed reading it, they could read about it here. The article was named:

DRUNKEN COWBOYS OF THE WORLD REJOYCE!

Three men were charged with violating the State of Pennsylvania's drunken driving law. One man was driving a pickup and the other two were riding horses away from a bar on a dark country road. The driver of the pickup allegedly rear-ended one of the horses.

DRUNKEN DRIVING THHROWN OUT

Unfortunately all three men failed sobriety tests, so all three were charged with drunken driving. The charge against the two men on horseback was thrown out after they argued before the State Supreme Court that the word "vehicle", in the states drunken driving law, does not apply to horses.

The prosecutors argued that the code specifically includes people riding animals. However the majority justices sited a similar case in Utah, where judges said that such a statute is confusing and too vague about which regulations would apply to animals as well as vehicles.

POETIC OPINION

One judge who is fond of writing rhyming opinions, summed up his one dissenting vote with these stanzas mimicking the theme song of the old T. V, show "Mr. Ed":

A HORSE IS A HORSE, OF COURSE, OF COURSE.
BUT THE VEHICLE CODE DOES NOT DIVORCE
IT'S APPLICATION FROM PERFORCE
A STEED AS MY COLLEGES SAID

IT'S NOT VAGUE, I'LL SAY UNTIL I'M HOARSE,
AND WHETHER A CAR OR TRUCK OR HORSE
THE LAW APPLIES WITH EQUAL FORCE
AND I'D REVERSE INSTEAD

According to what I found on the Internet, that once a law is on the books, it is hard to get it changed or removed. It seems that congress is too busy writing new laws to take the time to remove old laws that have become outdated.

An example of this kind of law is one about 'not spitting on the sidewalk.' That law was written eons ago when ladies all wore long dresses. It was to protect the hems of women's skirts as they drug along the sidewalks. Women no longer wear long dresses every day, and most of the time they ride in cars instead of getting around walking on the sidewalk. Yet the law remains.

The only way not to have thousands of inappropriate laws on the books is to add a clause stating when that particular law will expire.

MURPHY'S LAW
A temporary law never stays temporary, it goes ON, and On, and On....

CHAPTER FOUR

TRAVELOG

An older sister, Louise, and her husband, Roy, started a carnival. After running it some 20 years, they retired and sold it to my nephew and his wife, Dennis and Joanne Lynch. We went out with the carnival for several years after we retired. It was great fun.

OUR MANY TRAVELS

I should have named this column 'Travel Mishaps' because that is what I'm going to tell you about.

NEW ORLEANS

The first long trip that I remember is when we drove our old grey Plymouth to New Orleans. At that time we rented rooms at Motel Six at $8.95 per night. Gas was about $.50 per gallon and food prices were nominal.

The first trouble we ran into was when we stopped to buy fruit at a roadside stand. They displayed very good looking oranges and apples, but we soon found the stand was really a trap. The owner got Dan into a 'shell game' and had taken $100 from him before we wizened up and took off again for New Orleans. We were *'Small Town' People and showed it.*

BOURBON STREET

When we were walking down the famous Bourbon Street in New Orleans, we run into some friends from back home, Dr Thone and his wife, Leona. We had a good time running around with them and soon forgot about the $100 we'd lost.

Nothing else exciting happened on that trip unless you can count this: While walking down Bourbon Street, my husband and his friend spotted a long line in front of one establishment. Dan asked a guy what they were in line for and he told him they were waiting to have their shoes shined. Dan said that he would never stand in line that long just to have his shoes shined. The man said "you would if the shoe shine boys were topless shoe shine girls". I won't tell you if our crowd got in line or not.

BAD TRIPS

We've taken a lot of trips back and forth between Nebraska and Texas when bad things happened. Once we were pulling a trailer full of furniture when the tongue broke on the trailer and we almost lost all of our possessions. Another time we were traveling at night and towing our Nissan Station Wagon behind our motor home. The Station Wagon came unhitched in Topeka and we didn't miss it until we reached Oklahoma City.

MOTORHOME BROKE DOWN

One summer when we were heading north, the motor home broke down in Freer, Texas. We left it to be repaired and picked it up on our way back to Zapata in the fall.

REPLACED 5 TIRES

The last bad trouble I recall was when we were moving from Texas to Florida. Our motor home hadn't been driven for two years, so Dan had it checked over. The mechanic advised buying new tires, but Dan said he would take a chance on the ones we had. Some chance!

Before we got to Florida we had 5 flats and had bought the new tires after all, 'AND NOT AT DISCOUNT RATES.'

JOKE OF THE WEEK
It ain't over till it's over.

WHEREVER WE GO

FISH AND CHIPS

We are always changing or adapting our diet to what the locals eat where we are traveling. Sometimes we like their fare and sometimes we don't. When we went to England, it was the first time that we ate 'Fish and Chips.' That we really liked! Their fish was cooked crisp, and the 'chips' turned out to be just large 'French Fries.' Those were the best fries that we had ever eaten. We also found a soup bar where they served the most luscious 'basil tomato soup.' What we have bought or made ourselves after we came home have not tasted the same. Later we ran into 'Fish and Chips' again in Ontario, Canada. Probably they have as good here in the U.S., but they come under the name of 'Fish and Fries.'

COLD COFFEE

In Australia, I was introduced to 'Iced Coffee.' It was not just cold coffee with milk in it, but was made with real cream and great flavoring. I never found out what it was flavored with. You could buy it at any coffee bar and they even had it in machines like we buy our pop out of. Liking my morning coffee hot and black, I didn't expect to like it but I did. My efforts to duplicate it have fallen far short.

ALLIGATOR –*NO, NO, NO*

We camped through the 'OUT BACK' When we were in Australia.' We ate 'tea and crumpets there.' Now I always thought that crumpets were something like a cookie, crisp and sweet. What we were served with our tea was more like a big, white dinner roll. When our tour guide took us to one of Alice Springs fanciest restaurant, we were offered a meal of alligator or kangaroo. I cried 'Where's da beef?' and got it----I think!

POI

In Hawaii we went to a Luau. Most of the food was great but they wouldn't give up until we tried their *poi*, a starchy stem of the taro plant cooked and pounded until it becomes a paste. If you haven't tried it -----DON'T! Eat instead *kalua pig,* a young whole pig wrapped in leaves and roasted in a pit called an *ima*. It is delicious.

ATE AT BARS

In Wales it wasn't what you ate, but where you had to eat it. In the smaller towns at least, the bars were the only places that served food. So guess where we ate. The steaks, however, were very good. That was the only thing we felt comfortable ordering. Once in a while we did get very good vegetable soup.

IRISH STEW

In Ireland we didn't notice any difference in their food than ours except that they use a lot more potatoes. Their famous 'Irish Stew' is made with layers of potatoes, onions and mutton. It was very good.

THE BATTLE OF THE BEANS

When I grew up, our main staple was great northern navy beans flavored with bacon or pork hocks, onions and seasoning. We didn't hear of pinto beans until we moved to Texas. Even then we completely ignored them. Like grits, we knew that they were a southern favorite, but we thought the navy beans were better, so we kept on cookin' them up and eatin' them up.

Finally, after having pinto beans offered to us by some fine restaurants in Zapata, Texas, we were persuaded to try them. Their different taste began to grow on us. After a Mexican National gave me a recipe for pinto bean soup, I began to cook them as much as navy beans and like them more as time goes by.

FLORIDA'S MENU

When we moved to Florida, we were faced with more dietetic choices---*boiled peanuts, garlic fried peanuts* and *key lime pie*. I've only tried boiled peanuts once, I liked fried garlic peanuts right away and key lime pie would really upset my diet if I let it. It has become my favorite desert. We've learned to like grits also. I've experimented and came up with my own recipe. Believe it or not, instead of putting butter and a little salt on it, we use cream and sugar and eat it like cereal. What can I say? You know the old saying, "you can take the people out of the North but you can't take *all* the North out of people." or something like that.

JOKES OF THE WEEK

When the invisible man and the invisible women got married-they had children that weren't anything to look at either.

For some of us the wheel of fortune has a flat.

MAN-MADE MOUNTAINS

I had never heard of a man-made mountain, and this was the first time I'd ever seen one. Let me explain.

The end of my summer in Blair had come and we were heading to Florida via a route through Colorado Springs, Colorado. Our purpose was not to visit these mountains but rather to visit our 94 year old line dancing friend Thelma, and her daughter. Barbara.

CRIPPLE CREEK SLOTS

We discovered the mountains when our friend took us to Cripple Creek to gamble. We offered to drive, because after all, she was 94 years old. She would have none of that, because she *knew the way.* That she did! She took *the way* at what I felt was 90 miles an hour. We went along the few straight stretches, up hills, down hills and around the curves without slowing down. *We got there* and I loosed my tight grip on the seat. We did have a great time at the slots.

Of the four of us who played, our young friend, Thelma, was the only one who came out ahead. I guess she had learned something besides line dancing in her 94 years.

GOLD

On the way back to town, she took us on a guided tour through the mountains. This story really started way back in the 1890s when gold was discovered in California, Colorado, Alaska etc. I think you have all read about the 'gold fever' that struck thousands of people and made them rich over night. Among these people were the three Woods Brothers. They were realtors in the Victor and Cripple Creek areas until they struck gold, in 1892, while digging the foundation for a hotel. That discovery led to the famous 'Gold Coin Mine' which subsequently brought them much wealth and brought fame and wild growth to the area.

During the rest of the 19th century, there were 500 gold mines there, trains that carried the gold, street cars that carried workers to and from the mines, and 50,000 residents. Then as the gold seemed to peter out, gone were the mines, the train whistles and many of the residents.

ONE OF THREE CASINOS

During the 20th century the area came to depend on its wealth of gold mine History, its fantastic scenery and its 300 days of sunshine to draw people to the area as a great vacation spot.

It's hard to believe, but now a new or renewed glory has come to the area. First of all Cripple Creek was voted to become one of the three cities in Colorado to be allowed to have casinos. Now in another town named Victor, of streets paved with gold, today Victor's streets are lined with 100 year old buildings that stand as a legacy to the hustle and bustle of previous times.

AT LAST THE MOUNTAINS!!

There is a huge gold mining comeback in the area now!! The reason for it is that the 19th century gold miners were wrong. The gold was not all taken from the soil. It still holds at least 20% of its gold. No doubt, the 'old timers' had gotten out all the gold they could by using the methods that were available to them then. That 20% now is being taken out by new knowledge and therefore a new process. I can't explain the process to you, but I know the gold is separated from the soil by using strychnine. They have giant dump trucks hauling the used earth away and piling it up, thus building the MAN-MADE MOUNTAINS.

THOUGHT FOR TODAY

It ain't over 'til it's over.

Since I wrote this column Thelma Fatjo has passed away. She's sorely missed by my husband and my self.

RETIREES JOIN THE CARNIVAL

"ARE YOU STILL WITH THE CIRCUS?" For a long time that was the first greeting we'd get from our friends when we would return home after being gone for a while. I would politely explain to them: There are Circuses then there are Carnivals. Circuses have bearded ladies, high trapeze artists, lion tamers and beautiful ladies that ride elephants. I can assure you that I don't qualify for any of those jobs. There are Carnivals that have Merry-Go-Rounds, Ferris Wheels, Tilt-A-Whirls and Kiddy Rides. They have skill games and lots of food concessions. We went with a Carnival. My nephew and niece, Dennis and Joanne Lynch own one and they asked us to go with them for a summer when we retired. So we did!

BARKERS

Hit 'em in the head. knock 'em dead'! Three balls for a dollah! You get what you hit! Step right up little lady and ring the bell prize every time. The cries of the Carnival Barkers that rang out over the midway that summer still ring in our ears. Many stories have been told of young children who have run off to join a Circus or Carnival, with sometimes dire consequences. However let me show you *the other side of the coin* by telling you the tale of a grandma and grandpa who ran off with a carnival and had a wonderfully exciting and fulfilling experience.

Our careers did not afford us a good background for carnival work you say. However after raising three children and chasing three grandsons for years, we were ready for anything but the old rocking chair.

A GOOD BUSINESS

I admit, in the beginning we had some misgivings, but they were soon put to rest. Dennis and Joanne run a well organized business. Their ride boys have to meet a dress and hair code. Their concessions are owned and operated mostly by their friends and neighbors. Their sons, Mike and Dennis help them. The Carnival has always been a family affair.

THE POPPER

I worked mainly in the Popper, selling popcorn, pop, carmeled apples, snow cones and cotton candy to rosy faced children. Learning to make cotton candy was harder for me than learning to run the computer. Danny worked on the games. He did alright as long as he didn't spend too much time talking to the customers. Some of you know how Dan likes to talk.

We'll never forget the people we worked with or those we met all over Nebraska. Etched too in our memories are the indescribably beautiful sunrises we saw over the green grass and tree spotted terrain of Western Nebraska on our 6 A. M. moves.

THE PIED PIPER

After that first summer we were hooked. We followed the Calliope of the Merry-Go-Round for 10 years as though it were the sweet music piped by *"The Pied Piper of Hamlin."* However, unlike the children who followed the *"Pied Piper's"* music and disappeared into the mountain never to return, *WE FINALLY DID COME HOME.*

THE TRIP FROM H - - L

Our children became worried about our taking long trips in our car. They thought that airplanes were safer and faster. So we bought the plane tickets to go see our daughter in Texas for Christmas. What started out to be a nice holiday soon changed to 'The Trip from H - - L.

DAN RANG THE BELLS

We drove thirty miles from our home in Port St. Joe to the Panama City Airport and rented a car. We then drove the rental car and ours back to Port St Joe. The next morning we drove the rental car back to the airport and turned it in. We checked our luggage and then went through security. I had no trouble but my husband Dan set off all the bells. His heart defibrillator set them off. He was taken to another room and was checked out with a scanner.

THEN WE WAITED

Then we sat and waited for our 9;30 AM departure. So we waited and waited. They finally announced that our plane had mechanical problems and assigned us to a later time. I checked about every hour on the status of our plane. It had been out of the mechanical area, and then went back in. This happened 3 times. Finally they put us down for a time that missed our connecting flight in Atlanta by 20 minutes.

They could change us to a later flight to Atlanta that would get us to Austin at 9 PM. I balked. I had already called once to change our arrival time. They then offered to put us 'stand by' on a plane that had only one available seat. Believe it or not another seat became available and we took that earlier flight. Our 9:30 AM flight took off at 2:30 PM. We finally took off.

WE CAUGHT IT

That plane got to Atlanta just 20 minutes before our plane left for Austin, and we had 15 gates to go. Needless to say, we forgot our arthritis and ran; but we caught it.

When we got to Austin our suitcases weren't there. They had missed the last plane change, and were to be brought to New Braunfels when they arrived. We expected them the next day but they brought them at 3 AM and woke the entire RV Park up looking for us.

BRONCHITIS

We rested up 3 days before Cheryl's school vacation started. On the 4th day she got her vacation and we both got bronchitis. Talk about the 'sunny south' Texas wasn't it; not that year. It was cold and windy. We stuck it out 'til the week was up and then changed our plane ticket and came home a week early.

The trip back wouldn't have been so bad if we hadn't been sick. The ticket girl did give us the wrong gate number so we almost missed our flight in Austin. We were mixed up in Atlanta because I forgot we changed to Eastern Time there. We changed time twice more before we got to Port St. Joe. We were still sick for over a week.

Is flying better than driving? IT CERTAINLY WASN'T THAT TIME.

KENT BELOWS IN HIS STUDIO

CHAPTER FIVE

ODES & TRIBUTES

Kent Bellows was the typical small town boy who made it *BIG*. He was an artist when young, making posters for the school plays at Blair High School. His parents moved to Omaha for the last few of his high school years and he graduated there. He slowly worked his way to becoming a *great* artist who displayed his art all over from Omaha to New York City and in between. He died at the age of 56.

MY FRIEND KENT BELLOWS

Is it possible to be a friend to someone you have known only through his or her talent? If it is, I was a friend to Kent Bellows (2nd removed). I say this because I have never met him personally but I have been aware of his talent since he helped restore and move his father's painting of "The Last Supper". It was moved to the back to make room for the new organ they placed in the front of the Methodist Church Sanctuary years ago.

A FRIEND 2ND REMOVED

My son, Steve, had met Kent and was also good friends with David O'Hanlon who was in turn good friends with Kent. So, you see how I became a friend 2nd removed or is it 3rd? Steve has been a collector of Kent's art for a long time and is the one who sparked my interest in the first place. Steven and I both bought Kent's art through O'Hanlon.

I want to say at this time that I do not have any originals. What I have are photographs of paintings, lithographs, or prints of paintings. I don't care if they are not originals, I still enjoy them.

IT ALL BEGAN

The first works that I had of Kent's was an early painting, "The Sisters". (Photograph of a painting I think). It was of his two sisters. Steve bought me that for my birthday one year and this inspired my interest and love of his talent. Next I bought "Not of This Earth." (A print of a painting.) It was the combination of an old Chevy, a young couple, and a Flying Saucer. The next Bellows art that I added to my collection were two lithographs of cottonwood trees along the Missouri River. Then I bought a portrait of an unnamed Polish girl. (A photo of a painting.) "Rachel in White" (a poster made of a painting) dated 1988 was added.

I bought 2 prints of "Dirty Dishes". I leave one in Blair and have the other in my condo in Florida. I also have a signed book of copies that had been given out at one of Kent's shows in New York City.

KENT WAS HONORED

I am happy that they honored Kent the way they did recently in Omaha. I only wish that we had been in Blair then, so I could have gone to show my appreciation for all the joy his works have brought me.

(I wrote this column before he died. Then I wrote the following column after his death.)

WITH A STROKE OF THE CLOCK

It was with great shock that I saw Kent Bellows name in the Obituary Column. "Life is but the count of one". I don't know where that quote originated but it became clear to me what it meant. I couldn't believe it. With a second's stroke of the clock a life was gone taking with it a very rare talent.

BORN IN BLAIR

Kent grew up in Blair, Nebraska and spent a lot of his teenage years attending Central High School there. He was just a little older than my children were. My daughter, Cheryl said that he began his artwork at an early age making posters for the high school plays.

His parents moved to Omaha and he graduated from Burke High School there.

JOSLYN

We spend our winters in Florida leaving Blair about September 1st. Last fall, 2010, my son Steve, wouldn't let me leave until Kent's art show was on at Joslyn Art

Museum. We went opening day and I can say that I never have spent a more enjoyable afternoon. I, of course, saw pictures that I had never seen before. As you came in the door to the art show, there was a giant picture of "Sisters". Mine is a little 8 by 10. They displayed all of the pictures I have and many more.

I don't feel qualified to discuss Kent's artwork any further for fear of showing my ignorance. I don't pretend to be an expert of it, *----just a lover of it.*

Thank you Kent for all the joy your artwork has brought me.

Jean, Frank, Don, Ray, Cal, Corine, Pat, (not shown) Kay, Linda, and Sandy

ODE TO FRANK

HE LIVED 101 ½ YEARS

Frank Joseph Stukel was born in Menno, South Dakota on September 2, 1906. He died March 15, 2008 at 101 ½ years old. Frank and his three siblings spent their early childhood on the Stukel homestead north of Dixon, S. D. The family moved to Randolph, Nebraska in 1912 but moved back to the Gregory, S. D. area in 1920. Frank graduated from Gregory High School in 1925. After high school, Frank was employed in restaurants in Gregory and

Winner S. D. and eventually in Randolph S. D. where he met and married Margaret Farmer. They spent their early married years ranching near Lucas and farming in the Gregory area.

BOUGHT RESTAURANTS

It seems he liked the restaurant business better than ranching as in 1947 he bought Fern's Café in Gregory. In 1949 he and a partner bought the Corner Café and in 1956 he bought out his partner and merged the two cafes into one as the Frank's Corner Café. Throughout the years, 4 generation of Stukel's have worked in the café.

COMMUNITY WORK

In Gregory, Frank and Margaret were very active in community affairs. For many years, Frank was the only coach of the Midget and Teener's baseball teams. He was a member of the St. Joseph's Catholic Church for 87 Years. He was a member of the Knights of Columbus where he served in many positions: Grand Knight, District Deputy, State Deputy and finally was a Fourth Degree Knight.

RETIREMENT DAYS

After his retirement, Frank and Margaret spent their winters in Zapata, where they were involved in the church and Community. Frank worked with A.A.R.P. and served in many district and state positions. Margaret worked mainly for her church. They were fortunate to have many happy years of retirement in Zapata before Margaret died in 1996.

ENTERTAINING

We met him here in Zapata. He lived only a block from us. His son Ray also lived close. Among some the our happiest times in Zapata were the Fish Fries that Frank and Ray put on at Ray's house for the entire neighborhood and other friends. They would fry the fish and everyone else would bring a side dish or desert. Then we would sit until the wee hours talking.

Frank and Margaret loved to entertain family and friends. They were diligent card players. They would get together with their friends several times a week and play 'Hand and Foot.' I'm sorry that we were left out of that. We are not good card players.

BIRTHDAY PARTY

Frank has a very large family. Once, I think it was his 94th birthday, the family hired a bus in South Dakota, and about 40 relatives came to his birthday party here in Zapata. I think that they thought he couldn't last much longer but he sure fooled them.

AT THE END

When he began to fail this March the family began to gather in Gregory. They have one daughter who lives in England. Frank knew that she was on her way so the family felt that he was just waiting until she got here. He must have been right because she got here just the day before he died. He was surrounded by all 10 of his children to see him on his way. They even told him to mark the way for them to follow.

I feel blessed having known such a man. He gave his all to his family and his community. If I know Frank he will find many things to do for his new community.

MAX WEST
(BULL DOG)

I've just finished reading Max "Bulldog" West's Column. At least my husband told me "Bulldog" was his knick name. If not true, it wouldn't be the first time Dan got the truth screwed up a bit when he told me something. Max's nickname could be something like: "Patriotic Kid", "Straight Shooter", "Good Soldier" or "Dependable Guy". He is all of those things and more.

A FANTASTIC MILITARY CAREER

He writes a column once a month to keep us up on what the veterans are doing. He is the one who would know. He has held numerous offices in the Veterans organizations including State Commander for the VFW.

Max is constantly on the go from one meeting to another. He is a veteran of three wars. He was in the South Pacific in World War Two, served in the Vietnam War and was a parachutist in the Korean War. I think he must have landed wrong at least a couple of times, because his knees are suffering for it now. He had one eye damaged in Korea and was discharge at that time or he would probably still be in the service of his country. He _is_ still in the service of his country working hard for the Veterans who fought for it.

HIS FRIEND DAN

My husband Dan also served in the Pacific Theater in WW11. They never met there though. It's a good thing, because they would probably have ended up shooting at each other. They do get together for talks to reminisce. You couldn't imagine the tales they have to swap about that period of time.

We have known him for about 9 years. I don't ever think of Max without smiling. He has a sense of humor that won't quit. He and my husband, Dan always have something going. Dan kids Max about living so long just to keep Dan from marrying his wife Lila. I don't know what plans they have for me. They leave me out of the whole equation and I'm probably better off.

When they are not kidding about that, Max is chasing Dan and trying to get back the tools he has borrowed from him. That's one of Dan's faults. He would rather borrow a tool than look for one or buy his own. It's not that Dan's cheap; it's just one of his quirks—among many.

Max is a Nebraskan through and through. He was born in Neligh, lived for a while in Fremont and moved to Blair and has lived here since. Max has been very active in the VFW and has written a column for the Enterprise keeping Veterans up to date on what's happening in their world.

WORDS FROM WW11

SNAFU   = Situation normal: all fouled up
KILROY   = Kilroy was here
SADSACK   = Famous cartoon character
ERNIE PYLE   = Heroic war correspondent

(Since this column was written, both Max and Lela have passed away. Max is sorely missed in our block and is probably missed by the entire town of Blair and State of Nebraska.)

ODE TO EFFIE

COVERED WAGON

Effie first lived in Hickman, Nebraska near Lincoln. When she was just a small child, they moved to the Atkinson area via covered wagon. I can remember her telling that she and her little sister walked most of the way. She lived there until she was grown. She then married and moved to West Point, Nebraska. Her children were raised there.

FARM WIFE

She remarried and moved with her new husband to Winnebago and then to Iowa and became a farm wife. In those times the wives worked as hard as their husbands. At harvest time she cooked for the hired help and even took the place of hired men in the field if they could not hire enough help.

One time her husband broke his leg at corn husking time. She called her youngest son who was in the CCC (Civil Conservation Corp) to come home and help her. They worked 45 days straight and picked 10,000 bushels of corn. When they were paid at .05 cents per bushel, she had only enough to pay for the grocery bill and the medical bill for her husband.

RAISED EVERYTHING

When I say grocery bill it was usually only for flour, sugar and salt. Everything else was raised on the farm. Effie raised a garden and canned all the vegetables. They had cows, pigs and chickens to slaughter for meat and they kept a cow to milk.

BUTCHERING

The pig slaughter was quite an operation. They didn't waste a thing. Effie washed out the intestines and used them to stuff with home made sausage. Head cheese was stuffed in the stomach membrane. She also made blood pudding. The pork she fried and put down in the cold cellar covered with lard to preserve it. Some of the meat was smoked for ham and bacon.

When a cow was butchered, all of the meat was canned. The meat was even scraped off of the head then the rest was boiled and used for soup.

SEWING FACTORY

Later they moved to Sioux City and Effie worked at Alfs Sewing Factory to help pay for the house they bought. That's when I met her.

STRANGE EATING HABITS

The first thing I noticed about her was that she had strange eating habits. When I was invited to their house for dinner, it wasn't anything to see her eating chicken feet or the stuche of a turkey. Once when I came to her house, there was an awful stink. I heard giggles coming from the kitchen. When I found her she and her son were sitting at the kitchen table eating limburger cheese. You can't imagine how the old limburger cheese smelled. Needless to say, I didn't stick around long that day.

HAT'S OFF!

I really take off my hat to that generation. Effie, like many others of that day was not formally educated. She had only an elementary education, but she was smart. I learned a lot from Effie. You see, she was my mother-in-law.

BEAUTY AT ANY AGE

In most peoples minds beauty is associated with young beauty queens, movie starlets, models and T.V. stars. However three people that I have known have proved that beauty knows no age.

HAZEL

First there was Hazel Harris. Those who have known her realize that her beauty reached much deeper than her pretty face. It showed through in her faith, loyalty and love of her family and neighbors. She spent her working life educating. She taught my children and they all have fond memories of her. They remembered her for her patience and the love of learning that they passed on to her students.

After she retired, she donated her time to setting up a nature program for Desoto Bend on the Missouri River. She made quilts for the aids children and for the homeless. She made Teddy Bears for Blair's Fire Department to give to the little victims of tragic fires. She was one of my best friends, and I remember the beauty of a life well lived. I know I'm not the only one who misses her.

RACHEL

Another one who had a beautiful life was Rachel Craig. Her beauty was not only in her face but in her personality. She was well-known and well-liked by her neighbors. In fact we had appointed her as 'Mayor of the Neighborhood". She was my teacher as far as crafts and quilts were concerned. She also taught me much about the Indian Nation and had quite a few Indian picture and knick knacks in her house. Under her influence soon my apartment was filled with Indian Pictures, Dream Catchers, vases and books on Indian life. When she passed away, part of me seemed to go with her.

AGNES

Then there was Agnes Spann. She was my husbands aunt. Her home was in Atkinson, Nebraska, but she and her husband, Elmer, lived next door to us when we went to our winter home in Zapata, Texas. We traveled in the same social sphere if you can call our neighborhood group that. She was also a retired teacher who had left her mark on hundreds of children. She was older than the rest of us, but she didn't want to be left out of anything. We didn't want to leave her out either. If you invited her to go somewhere with the group, you needed to give her plenty of notice. She vowed that she needed plenty of time to make herself beautiful.

When she was ready to go, BEAUTIFUL SHE WAS! She had her make up on to perfection over her smooth skin. She vowed that soap never touched her face. Only the most expensive of creams cleaned it. There was nary a wrinkle that dared to blemish her youthful skin. She dressed in the latest fashions, wore silk hose and had never given in to "old lady shoes", although she was 80 years old.

Her favorite saying was:

"IT'S ALRIGHT TO BE OLD, BUT YOU NEEDN'T ACT OLD".

CHAPTER SIX

IN THE POT

I have columns that don't fit in any special category but I am fond of them and would like to have them in this book. Where to put them? That's the question. Therefore, I believe I'm going to pick them out and throw them in a great big POT for you to deal with. *Thanks!*

TOPS SAVED MY LIFE

At least it added a good ten or fifteen years to it, and I'm really enjoying those years now. I've put in my time working for someone else and now I do what I want to. I don't mean that I don't ever work, but I do the kind that I like and want to do. I sew and travel, visit my children and grandchildren, and best of all I have time to write.

MY TOPS CLUBS

In case you don't know what a TOPS CLUB is, it stands for "TAKE OFF POUNDS SENSIBLY". I belong to TOPS#FL217PANAMACITY but TOPS is International. When I travel, I can weigh in at most cities.

I have also belonged to #222 in Blair, NE. and #1311 in Zapata, Texas. I lived in Zapata and belonged to the Zapata club when I lost 55 pounds, reached my goal and became a KOPS, "KEEP OFF POUNDS SENSIBLY".

TURNING POINT

My turning point came when a Doctor at the Mayo Clinic told me I was killing myself by being heavy. At the time I suffered from high blood pressure, kidney problems and arthritis. Since I wanted a lot more time to spend with my children and grandchildren, I stuck to a diet and lost my weight between April 15 and December 19, 2001.

NATIONAL GRADUATION

After you reach your goal, you have your choice of graduating at Area level, at State level or at International level, I chose to graduate and became a KOPS at IRD 2002 International Recognition Days in Fort Collins, Colorado and have kept my KOPS status now for 10 years.

GOOD CLUB

TOPS is a good club to belong to if you need to lose weight. The dues are low and you have the back up and encouragement you need. You weigh in each week, spend your time with others who have the same problem that you do and get recognition for the weight you have lost. You can lose it. Remember the old saying ; *Where there's a will there is a way".* *IT REALLY APPLIES HERE*

PROJECTS UNFINISHED

Have you ever started a project that you never finished? Well I Have. –Quite a few! There are those projects that I start when I see a new type of craft. I'm very interested then lose my interest after I have bought the material to make it. There are also many more that I really want to finish but I start something else before that project is done and I don't get back to it.

QUILTS

For instances, I love quilts. I have finished many of those, but have many more that remain unfinished. I bought a beautiful unfinished quilt at a garage sale. I had only to put a last piece of goods around the outside and put on the border. I put the goods around the quilt but never got the border put on. It wasn't done by the time vacation time came so I put the quilt away. When we came back and I was going to finish it, I couldn't find it.

STARS

A friend and sewing partner of mine, Rachel Craig who is now deceased, made me six stars for the center of quilts. I only needed to put the squares on the quilt to finish the top. Those quilts meant a lot to me because Rachel made them to have something to do before she died. I have one quilt top almost finished but I have had the lot for 8 years and have not gotten any further. I really want to finish them, but every time I run into the stars I vow to get at them and then get started on something else. I promise you Rachel, I'll finish at least 2 of them this month. I wish there was someway of contacting her so she would know I kept my promise.

OTHER SEWING

There is other sewing that I work at here and there. I run into two blouses that are cut out and ready to sew, two pair of slacks I started to remodel when I lost weight, a velvet dress I was making for a convention two years ago, many half-done pillows, and many wall-hanging tops that remain back-less.

Everyone, I'm sure, has a few unfinished projects but none like mine. I should make a list of all my projects and tackle them one at a time but I probably never will. I'll see something that interest me more and drop what I'm doing at the time.

OUR LOVING GMC

To end this sorry missile, I'll tell you about our big project that we have been working on for 10 years. My husband, Dan and I have worked off and on to get our classic GMC Motor home ready to sell. When we started it needed just a few things fixed before we put it up for sale. We have fixed those things, but as casually as we work on it, we can't seem to keep up with the depreciation. It now needs new tires and a pump fixed among other things. Don't read this column and laugh. READ IT AND WEEP!

JOKE

There is a very fine line between "hobby" and "mental illness".

BY ANY OTHER NAME

PACK RATS

A rat doesn't always look like a rat, with slinky body, pinched face and long tail. Sometimes it looks almost human, like my husband Dan and I. The human kind are "pack rats." We are really batting 100, because in our household of two, there are two of us.

CHECKING FOR SALES

We race each other for the Thursday Newspaper, not to read the news but to see what garage sales are *playing* this weekend. If there aren't enough to keep us busy in town, there is also the surrounding area. When the next town recently had an *"all city"* garage sale, we spent the morning there and still didn't visit all the sales. We sometimes just cruise around to see if there are sales that weren't advertised in the paper.

SPLITTING WITH FULLNESS

Garage sales seem to be our main form of entertainment now. We even gave up square dancing. Worsening arthritis we blamed for that. However we can run to beat somebody to a sale. We now have the better of two worlds. We spend our winters in

Sunny Florida, and our summers in Nebraska. Both of our homes are splitting with fullness.

When we recently moved our *winter home* from Texas to Florida, we had four sales before we left and gave away a lot of things we didn't want to take with us. We still had a moving van and a truck to move when we came cross country.

MORE THAN WE NEEDED

We had to replace most of the furniture. That's all we needed, but we didn't stop there. We started going to garage sales to buy odds and ends and never stopped. We bought in Florida and bought in Nebraska and moved it all to our home in Florida where we had room. We thought! Now all our storage places are full, the walls are lined with pictures and furniture and we again have a garage so full that we can barely squeeze a car in.

ANTIQUE HORSE

Our Nebraska son, Steve and his wife Jeannie came down on vacation last March, when we were still in Florida. He has a van and he brought a few things down south for me that we just couldn't get along without. I repacked the things in the garage and made room for most of it there. He also brought my prized possession---the restored merry-go-round horse.

Let's see. To make room for the horse, I crowded things together on my East wall. Then I moved my chair and end table over there. Next I moved the chair and table lamp that sat in front of the south window to where my chair used to be. Then there was plenty of room to put the horse in front of the south window. It looks great there!!! But the rest of the living room looks crunched.

LET'S GO

Sorry! I have to end this column now. There are six garage sales advertised in the paper for this morning and Danny is yelling for me to get ready.

And so it goes. >>>>>>>>>

THE BUCKET LIST

DRIVING MISS DAISY

*Morgan freeman is one of my favorite actors. He is the black man who played in "Driving Miss Daisy". That was the first time he grabbed my attention, and I have remembered that movie ever since.

BUCKET LIST

*The next movie I saw him in was "The Bucket List". Both he and Jack Nicholson played lead parts. This movie is the story of two terminally ill men who decide to complete life's "to do" list before kicking the "bucket". This theme struck a cord with Freeman who has been keeping his own "bucket list" for years. First on his list was to escape from the poverty of his life on the cotton plantation of Greenwood, Mississippi. Then it was to somehow turn his life in the Air Force into an acting career. He accomplished both.

SAVED HIMSELF

*I read an article about him that told that 28 years ago he was navigating a sailboat to Bermuda. He ran into a storm that was so strong it had pummeled his boat to its side. He had two choices. He could stay in the cabin with his wife radioing for help that he knew wouldn't get there in time. Or he could go up and try to right the boat himself. He righted the boat and himself as well. That experience, he said, influenced the rest of his life. He realized that he could do most anything if he just tried hard enough.

YOU CAN'T HIDE

*He has already accomplished many things on his list. He loved to fly, so at 65 he learned to fly and bought himself a Cessna. He loves "Blues Music, so he opened a "Blues Club" in Clarkstown, Mississippi, near where he was born. In his career, he wanted to play parts other than criminals, so he worked his way into lead roles. As when he nearly died years ago sailing, he says "you can't just hide in the bottom of the boat and hope someone will save you. You have to go up and save yourself".

WORKED WITH NICHOLSON

*To work with Nicholson was another item on his list. That item was taken care of when Morgan co-starred with Jack in "Bucket List". If you saw that movie you should be convinced of having a list. I have always had one although I didn't have a name for it: To have a loving family, to have a good job, to graduate from college, to finally become a writer, to have my columns syndicated, and to write a book. I will never graduate because I have attended 8 colleges and have just 80 credits, but the rest of the list I have hopes of finishing. I'm writing that book now.

Let's all get a Bucket List started. As Morgan says at the end of the article:

"HOW CAN YOU EXPECT TO GO ON WITHOUT ONE?"

JUST THREE LITTLE WORDS

In the "Olden Days" when I was growing up, there was a song on the Hit Parade called "Three Little Words". It was very popular and played constantly on the radio. Everyone knew all the words because they owned the record. It was also our favorite song to dance to.

EXCUSE ME

About that time my mother was trying to pound into my head the importance of three other little words that she felt was important. The first of these words was *excuse* me. She said if I used that word every time I bumped into someone accidentally, crossed unintentionally in front of them, needed to interrupt their conversation, or in any other way I intended to intrude into anyone else's space, it would soon become automatic and make me many friends.

PLEASE

Another important word she felt was *please*. That little word she said could get me more than any amount of might or muscle. People that you used it on were left with a good feeling and were much more apt to give you what you were wanting. No one likes demands, so if you added please behind your request for something, you would be twice as apt to get their cooperation. Our demand would be changed to a request and it would change many a frown to a smile. Try it.

THANKS

There was a third word she felt would change your life if you used it whenever it was appropriate. That word is *thanks*. This, she felt was the most important because it brought a feeling of worth to the recipient and a feeling of goodwill to the giver. Believe me I know. I have done a lot of volunteering and the thanks I got meant more to me than money. There are so many ways that you can show thanks. Among them is that you can send a thank you card. Another is to make a quick phone call.

Use these three words often. You'll find they are very effective and that they never go out of style.

Another time you can say "thank you" is to your waitress as she fills your coffee. I know it is her job to wait on you but I know it makes her feel better to know her attention is appreciated. Her job isn't easy.

I LOVE YOU

Getting back to the old song, JUST THREE LITTLE WORDS, the three words in it were *I love you.* Use them occasionally on your friends. Use them often on those who love you and brought you up. You never know how long you'll have them around. Then if you sing better than I do, try singing it to them. I don't suggest that you sing it to the waitress unless you have a voice like Elvis Presley. I'm certain you could get a copy of the music at a music store.

JOKES OF THE WEEK

These days I spend a lot of time thinking about the *here after*. I go someplace to get something and wonder what I'm *here after*.

CHAPTER SEVEN

LAUGHTER, TEARS, LOVE & HATE

Tears are not always a bad thing; neither is hate. That's hard to believe isn't it? Wait! Love and Laughter are not always great. I'll show you. After you have read the following columns you'll understand what I am trying to say.

OPTIMIST

ACHES AND PAINS

I am by nature an optimist. I always see the cup half full instead of half empty. When I wake up in the morning full of aches and pains, I don't dwell on that. I know that the aches and stiffness will be gone as soon as I take my morning walk and my television exercises.

SELECTIVE MEMORY

I have a very selective memory. I always remember the good things that have happened to me and forget the bad. I had a relative that was just the opposite. She remembered everything bad that happened in the family and was constantly reminding everyone about them. Not only did her attitude make her miserable, but also she passed her bad mood on to everyone she talked to. When things aren't going just right with me, I remember what my father long ago taught me, "This too shall pass." And it does.

TEARS

There are times though, when I can't hold back the tears. They are my way of expressing deep emotion, and have nothing to do with being a pessimistic. I cry at funerals, weddings, births sad movies and at both "hellos" and "good byes". I sob with wronged heroines in soap operas, and laugh until I cry at T. V. comedians. Neither joy nor sorrow takes precedence in their ability to make me cry. My tears are as meaningless, endless and inevitable as the traditional babbling brook.

COMPASSION

In one instance, however, tears held great significance for me. That was the one time I saw my husband cry. Until that happened, I don't believe I really loved or understood him. Because he didn't show his emotions as outwardly as I did, he seemed to be quite unfeeling. It happened on a day that we attended a military funeral. Since it wasn't for anyone really close, I was astonished to see my husband break down. His tears were not easy. They came protesting from the depth of his emotions. For once I was dry eyed in my concern for him.

To this day I don't know if his tears were for the Marine in the casket or for all the friends he saw fall on the battlefields. However, in that instant, I realized that he had love and compassion for his fellow men, and the ability to cry for their suffering. I was never more proud of my husband.

Now, when life's stings leave me misty eyed, I lean on his strength and composure; yet feel warm in the knowledge that beneath his calm he is crying with me.

GREAT TRUTHS

*George Washington never told a lie, but he never had to make out a 1040.

*You can't please *all* of the people *all* of the time, but you can make them all angry at the same time.

"LOVE AND HATE"

In this life we run into both love and hate. Most of us claim that we embrace the LOVE emotion. We learned to "LOVE THY NEIGHBOR," "LOVE YOUR PARENTS", "YOUR SIBLINGS", "YOUR PETS" and your "HUSBAND". You'd be surprised though by how many things that you hate. Let me tell you about some things that bring very strong emotions to me.

Besides my, parents, my neighbors, my siblings my pets and my husband, there are many things that I love and enjoy. Here are a few of them:

I JUST LOVED IT:

*When Frank Sinatra walked on stage and sang "I'll Do It My Way".
*When I saw the beautiful sunset as I drove back to Zapata from the Valley.
*When my grandchildren came to visit.
*When my house filled with relatives and friends for a holiday dinner.
*When I got a letter from "anybody." Also when I got birthday cards. I love them!
*When my kids said "Mom that was the best meal!"
*When the soloist at church sang, "Amazing Grace"

*When Archie Bunker told his wife when she signed the income tax report, "You're in trouble clear up to your neck."
*When I went to line dancing in Zapata.
*When my children brought home an "A" on their report card.
*When they graduated from high school or college.
*When I graduated from high school. I never made it through college.

The word "hate" has a very bad connotation but there are times that "hate" does some good in the end. As an example there were women who hated it when a drunk driver killed somebody so they started the "MAD" (Mothers Against Drunk Drivers) Organization and much good has come of it. You don't think you hate anyone or? anything. Just listen to what I have hated.

I JUST HATED IT:

*When Johnny Carson died.
*When we went to war yet again and lost so many of our boys.
*When a politician I admire does something against the law.
*When I forget to set my alarm clock and oversleep.

*When I gain a pound or four and go out of my KOPS leeway. (All TOPS members know what I'm talking about.)
*When my television or computer goes on the fritz.
*When I'm late to church.
*When it is past time to vaccumn my floors or clean my windows.
*When the chicken burns and we have to go out for supper. (Come to think of it MUCH GOOD COMES OF THAT.)

JOKES OF THE WEEK

"Ninety eight percent of the adults in this country are decent, hard working, honest Americans, it's the other lousy two percent that get all the publicity. But then we elected them."

THE BEST PRESCRIPTION

"Once Upon A Time" a man wrote a book, and I read it. The book very well might have been a 'Fairy Tale'. I'll tell you about it and let you be the judge. I don't recall who the author was, but I didn't ever forget the message the book contained.

This man stated that he had gotten ill after breathing the fumes from the exhaust of an airplane that was taking off. It affected all his joints and therefore his motivation. The doctors who treated him weren't able to diagnose or cure the disease, so he decided to treat himself.

HIS PRESCRIPTION

In his research he found out about Vitamin C's curative powers. So he prescribed himself, four times its daily-requirements. Then he read about how laughter had a healing affect. So he bought all of the funny tapes that were available. They included 'The Four Stooges', 'Laurel and Hardy', 'Fibber McGee and Molly', 'George Burns and Gracie Allan'.

He took those tapes to his room and played them over and over laughing his head off. He diligently took the vitamin C. Visitors were restricted to those who had good news or a joke and left their troubles outside. He had the T. V. and radio taken from his room and didn't read the paper. He only left his room to go to the bathroom and to shower. His wife brought his meals.

'ABRA CADABRA' HE WAS WELL

For weeks that went on until his mood improved and his health became better. Finally all his symptoms were gone. He was convinced that it was his hilarious lifestyle plus vitamin C that did it. Maybe! Maybe not! but it's easy for me to believe in the healing powers of laughter.

THE FAIRY TALE

This winter I had an upper respiratory infection that just wouldn't go away. I had taken a chest decongestant, a nasal spray and took an antibiotic. After this regime for three weeks the infection was still with me. Then this book came to mind. So I bought a bag of vitamin C enriched cough drops and went to my room. I quit watching War News and other upsetting things on T.V. I began watching a channel that runs old tapes including Laurel and Hardy, Bing Crosby and Bob Hope (Road Shows) and Jack Benny and Rochester. I watched them until I was practically rolling on the floor with laughter.

After another week my respiratory infection was gone. Was it laughter or medicine that did the job? You decide. Was this whole column a 'Fairy Tale'? Whatever you believe, it won't hurt you to concentrate on the 'good news', smile at your neighbor once in a while and just remember to laugh often. 'Laughter never hurt anyone' and you'd be surprised how much better you and every one around you will feel.

JOKE OF THE WEEK

There is a theory that if a burglar is left alone; he soon becomes rich enough to retire.

LAUGH LOUD AND OFTEN

A friend asked me when I started writing columns, what they would be about. I answered (hopefully) that they were going to be humorous. Of course it probably wouldn't be a hearty laugh for everyone all the time, but I would try.

SADNESS

I feel there is too much sadness in the world today. We are exposed to it daily via television and newspapers, and we once in a while experience it in our own life. Occasionally we need to forget it all and have a good laugh.

HUMOR

Science studies show that humor has tremendous health benefits. Frequent belly laughs can guard against illness and can perhaps lengthen your life. Laughter helps you to breathe easier. It massages the heart and other major organs of the body, and improves the workings of the immune system. It seems that people who are able to find something funny in the dilemmas in their lives and have a good laugh, feel better faster than if they had a good cry.

OLD STYLE COMMEDIANS

It doesn't seem to me that there are as many plain comedians on today's television as their were on radio and early television. Maybe I'm just showing my age, but think of what we had: Fiber McGee and Molly, George Burns and Gracie Allen, Laurel and Hardy, Wheeler and Woolsey, Jack Benny and Rochester, Red Buttons, Lucille Ball and Desi Arnez, Will Rogers, Abbot and Costello, Milton Burl, Danny Kaye, Martha Rae, W. C. Fields, The Marx Brothers, Martin and Lewis, and even Johnny Carson. There is probably some I've left out. It seemed that there was always something to laugh at. Some of these guys I used to have on tape. I think I'll start looking for them again.

ONE MORE SMILE

If you want more friends, laugh more. My dad used to recite a poem that had the following lines:

Laugh and the world laughs with you.
Weep and you weep alone.
This brave old earth, must borrow its mirth.
It has troubles enough of its own.

It's true. No one likes a sad sack. That is part of the reason that I'll try to have something funny in all of my columns. I may be serious at times, but never sad or negative. You have my permission to laugh your head off. Even if you have heard the joke before, it is good for one more laugh.

JOKES OF THE WEEK

"Farmers Credo" Sow your wild oats on Saturday Night, then on Sunday pray for a crop failure.

The trouble with "life in the fast lane" is that you get to the other end in a hurry.

"A bridge over troubled waters" is probably not a good place to fish.

CHAPTER EIGHT

MOM AND DAD'S SHOWS

My dad had a one-man show of funny songs, jokes, guitar solos and recitation. He 'played' the Midwest at school houses, opera houses and even street corners. He walked up and down the street using a megaphone to advertise the show. Entertainment then was scarce so he always had a 'full house' or a packed street.

My mom wasn't much of an entertainer but where dad went, like Ruth in the bible, mom would follow helping whenever she could. Dad finally let her in his show. She recited a couple of simple poems and they sang a duet together.

MOM

Mom's world was following Dad. When my parents were first married they traveled to his 'One-Man Show' on a motorcycle with a side car. When Dad discovered that the motorcycle scared the cows, he bought a Model A Ford for use instead.

When the kids started coming Mom became a 'stay at home Mom'. Although we hadn't much financially, she always worked at giving us a happy childhood.

MOM'S LIFE

GRANDPA

Mom was born in Onawa Iowa to Cora and Orville Sampson. All I know about her father, my grandfather, was that he worked as a fireman. He was tall and slim and was on the firemen's foot racing team. The last we knew a picture of the firemen's team still hung on the wall at the Onawa Fire Department. I only remember seeing my grandfather twice. He died of cancer while quite young. I was too young to remember much except that they had moved to Sioux city before he died.

GRANDMA

Grandma was as short as he was tall. She was a widow for a long time. She made all my school clothes so I saw a lot of her and we were very close. I thought that she was the smartest and the most self sufficient woman that I've ever known. She worked at home and made her living by laundering curtains for rich people. She washed, starched and dried them on what she called a stretching frame. In those days there wasn't any welfare to take care of old people. Everyone took care of themselves.

ALONG CAME DAD

My mother lived a quiet and uneventful life until a dashing entertainer, my father, came along and swept her off her feet. He gave entertainments at small towns around Onawa until he had wooed and wed the little blue eyed damsel who was my mother, Edna Sampson.

He swept her off her feet and onto a motorcycle with a sidecar that they used to go from place to place giving his one-man show. He gave his entertainment at School Houses, Opera Houses, and as a last resort on a street corner. He advertised by going around the streets with a megaphone.

MOM'S PART

They didn't have much for entertainment in those days, so they always had a full house. Dad's Repertoire consisted of funny songs, jokes and recitations like: "The Raven" and "Little Orphan Annie". Mom put her two cents in by reciting simple poetry. For example:

A wise old owl sat in an oak,
The more he heard, the less he spoke,
The less he spoke the more he heard.
Why aren't we all, more like that bird?

As you can see, Mom wasn't much of an entertainer, but she was always there for backup to dad.

BATHURST SINGERS

That all ended when we kids started coming. Mom, of course, stayed home and took care of us and Dad went back to his one-man show. There were 6 kids, 2 boys and 4 girls. I was fifth from the oldest. As we kids grew up, we joined Dad's show and finally formed a family chorus. 'The Bathurst Family Singers.' They wouldn't let me in the chorus. They said I was too young but I soon learned it was because I couldn't sing. They did let me dance in the show. I loved that. My younger sister had a wonderful voice. She soon stole the show.

We could only go with Dad in the summer because of school. It was hard to hold a chorus together as we got older, so Dad went back to his one-man-show and Mom cooked, and washed and cleaned the house and took care of six kids.

I feel that I am really blessed. I have nothing but good memories of my parents.

MOM'S ADVICE TO ME

One thing I learned when I was very young is that there is more than one way of doing something. One of my mother's favorite saying was: "*There's more than one way to skin a cat*". I don't know how she knew that. She didn't ever skin one or kill a chicken or kill a fish. To my knowledge she didn't ever hurt a living thing. She did know that people did things in different ways. When I was young I believed everything she said so I grew up with the same beliefs.

LEAVING

As I grew older I learned that there was quite a few different ways that a marriage or relationship could break up. I knew this because it was pounded into my head by the musical words of Paul Simon his song that went; 'THERE ARE FIFTY WAYS TO LEAVE YOUR LOVER'. I learned this by listening to the song, not by personal experience. My husband, Dan, has been around for a long time. I can't say the neither of us had a fleeting thought about leaving in all that time.

TURKEY TALK

Probably there are more ways than 50 to prepare a Christmas Turkey. Now I haven't tried them all.

I'm a traditional cook that roasts the turkey at 325 degrees stuffed with sage dressing. I seal it in tinfoil until the last 30 minutes, then open it up and let it brown.

CAJUN WAY

There's the Cajun Way. You cook a 12 pound turkey for 500 degrees for just an hour and a half. Some people grill, deep fry, microwave, or even smoke them. Then there is the new way, Turducken. Here's the recipe:

TURDUCKEN

BUY A TURKEY, DUCK AND CHICKEN
PUT THE DUCK INSIDE THE TURKEY
PUT THE CHICKEN INSIDE THE DUCK
STUFF THE CHICKEN WITH DRESSING
ROAST ALL TOGETHER UNTIL DONE.

They say it tastes great! I can't wait until next Christmas to try it. I know my mother would welcome this recipe were she here today.

WHEN YOU WORE A TULIP
(MOM AND DAD'S DUET)

WHEN YOU WORE A TULIP,

A SWEET YELLOW TULIP,

AND I WORE A BIG RED ROSE.

WHEN YOU CARRESSED ME,

'TWAS THEN HEAVEN BLESSED ME,

'TWAS A BLESSING NO ONE KNOWS.

YOU MADE LIFE "CHEERY",

WHEN YOU CALLED ME "DEARY",

'TWAS DOWN WHERE THE BLUE GRASS
GROWS.

YOUR LIPS WERE SWEETER THAN JULEP,

WHEN YOU WORE A TULIP,

AND I WORE A BIG RED ROSE.

ROLAND JAY BATHURST
VERSATILE ENTERTAINER

ELOCUTIONIST AND IMPERSONATOR, SERIOUS, SENTIMENTAL AND HUMOROUS SELECTIONS MINGLING THE SMILES WITH THE TEARS.

You will laugh

'till you cry at

his serio-comic

impersonations

His serious

themes appeal

to the pure

Noble tender

emotions of the

human heart

MR. BATHURST HAS A STYLE OF ENTERTAINING THAT GIVES HIS LISTENERS A SPIRITUAL UPLIFT AS WELL AS AN OPPORTUNITY TO ENJOY AN ENTERTAINMENT OF CLEAN, WHOLESOME AMUSEMENT

DAD'S ENTERTAINMENT

My Dad had a one- man show of funny songs, jokes, guitar solos and recitations. He played the Midwest at schoolhouses, opera houses and as a last resort on a street corner. He advertised by walking the streets with a megaphone and giving out 'show bills'. Entertainment was not plentiful in those days so he always had a FULL HOUSE

WRITE IT DOWN

DAD

My Dad was an entertainer and an elocutionist. I've been thinking a lot about him recently and would like to share a bit of him with you. He was a self-taught man. Since his dad was a farmer, naturally, he was kept home in the spring to plow the fields. He often laughed and said that he obtained his education at the end of the cornrows. He would take his schoolbooks to the field and stop at the end of the rows and read them so he could keep up with his class.

TEACHER

He was a trained teacher "in the beginning" of his career. It took only Normal Training and 8th grade to qualify. He hadn't taught long when he decided that teaching was a little tame for his wandering soul, so he joined a minstrel show. He had taught himself the guitar and the violin and had a good singing voice.

ENTERTAINING CAREER

That was the beginning of his entertaining career. After his experience with the minstrels, he devised a show of his own. He traveled across the country booking it in schoolhouses and auditoriums. He had a one-man show of stories, funny songs and recitations.

REPERTOIRE

His mother had started him on memorization. Thinking back, I'm amazed at the things he had memorized. His Repertoire included "The Raven" by Edgar Allen Poe, "The Charge of the Light Brigade", by Lord Alfred Tennyson, and "A Chariot Race". I don't remember the author. He also memorized fun poetry and sang funny songs. Two of his poems were "Little Orphan Annie" and "The Nonsense Rhyme". Two of his funny songs were: "The Little Old Ford It Rambled Right Along," and "They Gotta' Quit A Kickin' My Dog Around." He used all these in his shows.

MARRIED LIFE

He met and Married Edna Sampson from Onawa, Iowa and they had 6 children. The show eventually included the entire family. All my brothers and sisters had beautiful voices, so they had a family chorus but they wouldn't let me sing - they let me dance with the band instead. I can remember, dad teaching me how to clog. The entire show could only travel in the summer since we went to school.

HE FOLLOWED HIS DREAM

Perhaps that is where I got my wandering foot. I had been in at least 30 states when I was young. As we children got older, it was hard to hold the show together, so Dad went back to his one-man show and traveled alone. Eventually he took up photography so he could be home all the time with his family. He couldn't work for anyone else. He "danced to a different drummer" and "followed his own dreams".

One of my favorite nephews, Dickey, started me on the trek of "remembering dad" and I thank him much. He had always admired his grandfather's talent and intellect and I was the only one left to remember. Let that be a lesson to others. You have a wonderful gift in your memory. Write it down and leave it to posterity.

MY ANCESTRY

I have never researched my ancestry. A gentleman who was related to my Dad's brother got our name someway and contacted me. He sent me what he had researched about the Bathurst family and how they had come to America. Most of his findings, however, were from his side of the family.

SIR FRANCIS BATHURST

I did learn however, the first Bathurst here was "Sir Francis Bathurst". He had quite an estate but lost his Noble Standing when he took the American side in the Revolutionary War. If that hadn't happened my Dad would have been an Earl. I don't know what that would have made me. But I'm happy the way I am.

Besides English, my Dad told us we were also part Irish, Scotch, Welch, German and Dutch. I have always been proud of my ancestry. If I did not inherit something good from each group, I would not be the person I am. Not bragging!

MY DAD'S NOSE

My Dad had a Jewish nose, so he also, laughingly claimed to be German Jew. Thus he said, like the

Jewish People we children should all be good at business. However, my Mom told me he got his large curved nose by having a fight with our neighbor. I don't know who won, but Dad came out with a broken nose. Thus his claim to be Jewish.

THE IRISH

My parents always claimed that we kids learned our work ethics from their father. However that was only partially true. I believe we inhered it mostly from our Irish Ancestors. They were always "The Workhorses." They were the ones to be hired to do the work of those less active. The Irish were also great drinkers. I'm glad to say that they didn't pass that trait on to me. I can't say that about some of my family.

THE SCOTCH

What comes, I'm sure, to every ones mind, is that the Scotch is very "close with a penny". So am I. I put off buying something I really need until I see it on sale. I also am very fond of garage sales. My husband says I am "too fond." They have made me a pack rat. At the time I'm really convinced that I need the things I buy. Blame it on my ancestors. I'm just spending my pennies instead of pinching them.

THE WELCH

I have often wondered what in the world I could have inherited from the Welch. Little did I know that they would turn out to be one of my biggest contributors? I read today that Wales has been a land of poets and singers that dates back to the middle ages. I came from a family of singers and dancers and I love to write poetry. How about that?

GERMAN

My husband, who is German, says the most intelligent of my ancestors were the German. He also said they were the greatest inventers. That may be true but his view may have been tainted by the fact that his stepfather was one of them and very fluent in their language.

The only thing in German that I learned from him was a Drinking song. I loved to sing that song to make my mother angry. She was strictly a non-drinker.

THE DUTCH or NETHERLANDERS

I know that I inherited my love of Art from the Dutch.

Among the lists of their great artists were Van Gogh and Rembrandt. I don't own even prints of those two. I do have a black and white kitchen in Florida filled with black and white prints of Ansel Adams and Kent Bellows, a Nebraska boy who made good. Before he died he was showing his art at studios from Omaha to New York City.

"The Story of Ann Frank", and of the Little Boy who saved the Netherlands by sticking his finger to close a hole in a leaky dyke, is among the well-read writings of the Dutch People. Perhaps I inherited my love of writing from them.

BACK TO THE JEWISH PEOPLE

Come to think of it we were pretty good at business. Real Estate was our thing and we were fairly successful at it. Our daughter Cheryl followed our lead and our two sons Daniel and Steve followed suit.

I GUESS WE DID INHERIT SOMETHING FROM MY DAD'S NOSE

SOME OF ROLAND JAY BATHURST'S REPERTOIRE

FUNNY SONGS
You Gotta' Quit Kickin' My Dog Around
The Girls in Our Town

FUNNY VERSES
Everybody Thinks I'm Crazy But I Hain't
If I Could Be By Her

SERIOUS VERSES
Tell Me Not in Mournful Numbers
If I Should Die Tonight
The Day Is Cold, and Dark, and Dreary
*****

These offerings are over 100 years old.
The authors are unknown by me..

MY FAVORITE RECITION OF HIS WAS 'THE RAVEN'
BY: Edgar Allen Poe

'The Raven' is too long to be included in my book, but it is worth looking up at your library. I would sit time after time listening to him practice, and I'd never tire of hearing it. I often thought what a wonderful, intelligent, and talented father I had.

YOU GOTTA QUIT A KICKIN' MY DOG
AROUND

ME'UN LEM BRIGGS AND OLD BILL BROWN
WE TOOK A LOAD 'A CORN TO TOWN
AND OLD JIM PUP THE ORNERY CUSS
HE JUST KEP' A FOLLER'N US

AS WE WENT PAST MEL JOHNSON'S STORE
PASLY APPS CROWD CAME OUT THE DOOR
AND WHEN JIM STOPPED TO SMELL A BOX
THEY SHIED AT HIM A BUNCH OF ROCKS

CHORUS

EVERY TIME I COME TO TOWN
THE BOYS KEEP A KICKIN' MY DOG
AROUND
MAKES NO DIFFERENC IF HE IS A HOUND
THEY GOTTA' QUIT A KICKIN' MY DOG
AROUND

THEY TIED A TIN CAN TO HIS TALE AND
RUN HIM A PAST THE COUNTY JAIL
AND THAT PLUMB NATURALLY MADE ME
SORE
AND BILL HE CUSSED AND JIM HE SWORE

WELL WE JUMPED DOWN AND THERE
AND THEN
WE LIT INTO THOSE GENTLEMEN
AND WE SOON FILLED THE COURTHOUSE
SQUARE
WITH RAGS AND TEETH AND HIDE AND
HAIR

CHORUS

EVERY TIME I COME TO TOWN
THE BOYS KEEP A KICKIN' MY DOG
AROUND
MAKES NO DIFFERENCE IF HE IS A HOUND
THEY GOTTA QUIT A KICKIN' MY DOG
AROUND

AS WE WENT PAST THE COURTHOUSE
SQUARE

THE GIRLS IN OUR TOWNS

I'LL SING YOU A SONG OF THE GIRLS IN OUR TOWN,
YOU'LL ADMIT IT'S A POPULAR DITTY.
IT'S NOT VERY SHORT AND IT'S NOT VERY LONG,
BUT THE CHORUS IS CERTAINLY PRETTY.

-CHORUS-
FAL DITTA LAL, FAL DITTA LAL,
FAL DITTA LAL, DITTA LADDY.
FAL DITTA LAL, FAL DITTA LAL,
FAL DITTA LAL, DITTA LADDY.

SUZANNE WENT OUT TO MILK THE COW,
BUT WHEN SHE GOT THERE SHE DIDN'T KNOW HOW.
THE OLD COW THOUGHT SHE WAS TRYING TO TEASE
HER,
BECAUSE SHE MILKED HER WITH A LEMON SQUEESER.

-CHORUS-
THERE WAS A YOUNG GAL FROM LYNN,
WHO WAS SO EXCEEDINGLY THIN,
THAT WHEN SHE ASSAYED TO DRINK LEMONAIDE,
SHE SLIPPED THROUGH THE STRAW AND FELL IN.

-CHORUS-
THERE WAS A YOUNG GAL FROM DECATUR,
WHO TRIED TO SING IN A THEATRE.
BUT THE POOR LITTLE THING, WHEN SHE GOT UP TO
SING,
SHE GOT HIT BY A ROTTEN TOMAT'ER

-CHORUS-
THERE WAS A YOUNG GIRL FROM STELLA,
FELL IN LOVE WITH A BOWLEGGED FELLA'.
SHE TRIED ONE NIGHT TO SIT ON HIS LAP,
AND SHE FELL CLEAN DOWN IN THE CELLAR.

-CHORUS-
THERE WAS A YOUNG GIRL FROM OHI'R,
WHO TRIED TO SLIDE DOWN A BARBWIRE.
I DON'T THINK IT BEST, TO TELL YOU THE REST,
BUT THE FLAGS ARE HALF MAST IN OHI'R.

IF I COULD BE BY HER

I GOT A GIRL OVER TO TOWN
AND I DON'T CARE HOW THE ROBIN SINGS
OR HOW THE ROOSTER FLAPS HIS WINGS
OR WHETHER IT SHINES OR WHETHER IT
POURS
OR HOW HIGH UP THE EAGLE SOARS
IF I COULD BE BY HER

AND I DON'T CARE IF THE PEOPLE SAY
THAT I'M WEAK-MINDED EVERY WAY
AND NEVER HAD NO COMMON SENSE
I'D CLIMB THE HIGHEST PICKET FENCE
IF I COULD BE BY HER

YOU SEE SHE WEIGHS AN AWFUL PILE
BUT I DON'T CARE, SHE'S JUST MY STYLE
AND ANY FOOL CAN PLAINLY SEE
THAT SHE'D LOOK WELL BY THE SIDE OF ME
IF I COULD BE BY HER

WELL IT'S ALL ARRANGED FOR CHRISTMAS
DAY
CAUSE THEN WE'RE GONNA RUN AWAY
AND SOMETH'N THEN THAT COULDN'T BE AT
ALL BEFORE WILL THEN YOU SEE------
CAUSE I'LL BE BY HER

EVERYBODY THINKS I'M CRAZY

EVERY BODY THINK I'M CRAZY BUT I 'HAINT.
ANYBODY WHO KNOW ME
SAYS I'M THE SMARTEST ONE IN OUR FAMILY.
OF COURSE I'M THE ONLY ONE IN OUR FAMILY.

JUST TO SHOW YOU HOW SMART I AM
ONCE I PICKED UP A RED HOT IRON
AND I LAID IT RIGHT DOWN AGAIN WITHOUT
ANYBODY TELLING ME TO
AND I'M ONLY 21 YEARS OLD.
OF COURSE I WOULD HAVE BEEN 22
BUT I WAS SICK FOR A YEAR.

I HAD A BROTHER ONCE A LONG TIME AGO.
HE'S DEAD NOW
ME AND HIM WAS TWINS AND WE LOOKED
SO MUCH APART YOU COULDN'T TELL US
ALIKE.
YOU COULDN'T TELL US ALIKE WE LOOKED SO
MUCH APART, I MEANT TO SAY.

EVERY TIME HE'D DO SOMETHING MEAN
THE FOLKS WOULD LICK ME
CAUSE THEY COULDN'T TELL THE DIFFERENT.
I FOOLED 'EM ONCE
ONCE WHEN WE WERE LITTLE BOYS
I DIED AND THEY BURRIED HIM.

"TELL ME NOT IN MOURNFUL NUMBERS"

TELL ME NOT IN MOURNFUL NUMBERS

LIFE IS BUT AN EMPTY DREAM

AND THE SOUL IS DEAD THAT SLUMBERS

AND THINGS ARE NOT WHAT THEY SEEM

LIFE IS REAL, LIFE IS EARNEST

AND THE GRAVE IS NOT ITS GOAL

"DUST THOU ART TO DUST RETURNETH"

WAS NOT SPOKEN OF THE SOUL

NOT ENJOYMENT AND NOT SORROW

IS OUR DESTINED END OR WAY

BUT TO ACT THAT EACH TOMORROW

FINDS US FARTHER THAN TODAY

LET US THEN BE UP AND DOING

WITH A HEART FOR ANY FATE

STILL ACHIEVING, STILL PERSUINGS

LEARN TO LABOR AND TO WAIT

IF I SHOULD DIE TONIGHT

IF I SHOULD DIE TONIGHT MY FRIENDS WOULD

LOOK UPON MY QUIET FACE,

BEFORE THEY LAID ME IN MY RESTING PLACE,

AND DEEM THAT DEATH HAD LEFT ME ALMOST FAIR.

AND LAYING SNOW WHITE FLOWERS AGAINST MY HAIR

WOULD SMOOTH IT DOWN WITH TEARFUL
TENDERNESS,

AND FOLD MY HANDS WITH LINGERING CARESS -

THOSE HANDS SO EMPTY AND SO COLD TONIGHT.

IF I SHOULD DIE TONIGHT, MY FRIENDS WOULD

PRESS THEIR KISSES ON MY COLD DEAD BROW.

MY WAY IS LONELY, LET ME FEEL THEM NOW.

I AM TATTERWORN – MY FALTERING FEET ARE PIERCED

WITH MANY A THORN. THINK GENTLY OF ME,

FORGIVE OLD FRIENDS, FORGIVE I PLEAD.

WHEN DREAMLESS REST IS MINE I SHALL NOT NEED

THE TENDERNESS FOR WHICH I LONG TONIGHT.

"THE DAY IS COLD AND DARK AND DREARY

THE DAY IS COLD, AND DARK AND DREARY.

IT RAINS AND THE WIND IS NEVER WEARY.

THE VINES STILL CLING TO THE MOLDERING WALL,

AND AT EVERY GUST THE DEAD LEAVES FALL,

AND THE DAY IS DARK AND DREARY

BE STILL SAD HEART AND CEASE REPINING.

BEHIND THE CLOUDS IS THE SUN STILL SHINING.

THY FATE IS THE COMMON FATE OF ALL.

INTO EACH LIFE SOME RAIN MUST FALL,

SOME DAYS MUST DARK AND DEARY.

EPILOGUE

SHE'S DONE IT ALL

The author was born in Sioux City, Iowa the daughter of wonderful parents and had an enjoyable and interesting childhood. She was blessed with 3 wonderful children, 3 grand children, 2 great grand children and the same husband for 65 years.

She had a good career with Northwestern Bell Telephone Company, now Quest. After she and her husband retired they moved South for their winter home.

Next they traveled to Alaska and Hawaii and took jaunts to many foreign countries. They visited Ireland, South Korea, England, New Zealand, Wales, France, Germany, the Netherlands, Canada, Australia and was all over Mexico.

Between traveling with her Dad growing up and with her husband later, she's been in 40 of the 50 states of the good old U. S. of A. With her Dad she's swam in Salt Lake where you can't sink, walked down the Grand Canyon seen Old Faithful Geyser erupt, gone up Pikes Peak in a Model T Ford, went through Wind Cave, and many more places that she hasn't time to mention. Gotta get this book published. She has 7 more to write and she's already 89 YEARS OLD.

AUTHOR

VIRGINIA BATHURST BECK was born in 1923 in Sioux City, Iowa. She is now a very young 89. She and husband Dan have lived in 4 states: Iowa, Texas, Nebraska and now winters in Florida. Her columns come from her memory, letters and her computer. They bring you from the Great Depression to the present. This is the 2nd of 8 books she intends to write.

!!WISH HER LUCK AND A LONG LIFE!!